FINANCIAL LINKAGES, REMITTANCES, AND RESOURCE DEPENDENCE IN EAST ASIA

FINANCIAL LINKAGES, REMITTANCES, AND RESOURCE DEPENDENCE IN EAST ASIA

Editors

Takuji Kinkyo
Kobe University, Japan

Takeshi Inoue
Nanzan University, Japan

Shigeyuki Hamori
Kobe Unlversity, Japan

World Scientific

W JERSEY · LONDON · SINGAPORE · BEIJING · SHANGHAI · HONG KONG · TAIPEI · CHENNAI · TOKYO

Published by

World Scientific Publishing Co. Pte. Ltd.

5 Toh Tuck Link, Singapore 596224

USA office: 27 Warren Street, Suite 401-402, Hackensack, NJ 07601

UK office: 57 Shelton Street, Covent Garden, London WC2H 9HE

Library of Congress Cataloging-in-Publication Data
Names: Kinkyo, Takuji.
Title: Financial linkages, remittances, and resource dependence in East Asia / Takuji Kinkyo,
    Kobe University, Japan, Takashi Inoue, Nanzan University, Japan,
    Shigeyuki Hamori, Kobe University, Japan.
Description: New Jersey : World Scientific, 2015. | Includes bibliographical references and index.
Identifiers: LCCN 2015027953| ISBN 9789814713399 (hardcover : alk. paper) |
    ISBN 9814713392 (hardcover : alk. paper)
Subjects: LCSH: Emigrant remittances--East Asia. | Finance--East Asia. |
    East Asia--Economic conditions.
Classification: LCC HG3976.5 .K56 2015 | DDC 332/.042095--dc23
LC record available at http://lccn.loc.gov/2015027953

British Library Cataloguing-in-Publication Data
A catalogue record for this book is available from the British Library.

In-house Editor: Philly Lim

Typeset by Stallion Press
Email: enquiries@stallionpress.com

Printed in Singapore

Contents

About the Editors

Takuji KINKYO is a Professor of Economics at Kobe University in Japan. He received his PhD from School of Oriental and African Studies, University of London. He previously worked as Director, International Department at Ministry of Finance, Japan. His research interest includes exchange rate economics, finance and development, and Asian economic integration. His work has been published in leading academic journals. He is the co-editor of *Global Linkages and Economic Rebalancing in East Asia* (World Scientific, 2013) and *Financial Globalization and Regionalism in East Asia* (Routledge, 2014) .

Takeshi INOUE is an Associate Professor of Policy Studies at Nanzan University in Japan. He received his PhD from Kobe University. He previously worked as Research Fellow at Institute of Developing Economies (IDE-JETRO). His research interests include Indian macroeconomy, financial inclusion and remittances. He is the co-author of *Indian Economy: Empirical Analysis on Monetary and Financial Issues in India* (World Scientific, 2014).

Shigeyuki HAMORI is a Professor of Economics at Kobe University in Japan. He received his PhD from Duke University and has published many papers in refereed journals. He is the author or co-author of *An Empirical Investigation of Stock Markets: the CCF Approach* (Kluwer Academic Publishers, 2003), *Hidden Markov Models: Applications to Financial Economics* (Springer, 2004), *Empirical Techniques in Finance* (Springer, 2005), *Introduction of the Euro and the Monetary Policy of the European Central Bank* (World Scientific, 2009), *Rural Labor Migration, Discrimination, and the New Dual Labor Market in China* (Springer, 2014), *Indian Economy: Empirical Analysis on Monetary and Financial Issues in India* (World Scientific, 2014), and *The European Sovereign Debt Crisis and Its Impacts on Financial Markets* (Routledge, 2015).

List of Tables

List of Figures

Introduction

The dynamism of the East Asian economy is closely related to the region's real economic linkages through foreign trade and foreign direct investment (FDI). The deepening of real economic linkages has been the key driving force for East Asia's rapid industrialization and economic growth. Multinational enterprises' global supply chains have spread extensively across national borders, connecting the East Asian economies [Ando and Kimura, 2005], and developing Asian economies have been able to accelerate the process of industrialization by participating in these supply chains [Gill and Kharas, 2007].

By comparison, East Asia's financial linkages through cross-border financial transactions were lagging. However, East Asia has witnessed a dynamic and multidimensional development in international financial linkages over the past decade. Between 2001 and 2013, cross-border portfolio investment liabilities increased by more than seven times in non-Japan East Asia (IMF Coordinated Portfolio Investment Survey). This is presumably due to domestic capital market development and greater openness to capital flows. Consequently, the correlation of stock market returns increased significantly not only between Asia and the US, but within the East Asian region as well [Kinkyo and Hamori, 2014]. Stronger cross-border financial linkages can promote the development of domestic financial markets in terms of efficiency, liquidity, and transparency [Prasad and Rajan, 2008].

However, the global financial crisis of 2007–2009 has revealed the pitfall of the deepening of international financial linkages. The rapid spread of financial turbulence across national borders has demonstrated that no country can escape the menace of the financial tsunami caused by mega-scale shocks in the financial center. It is no coincidence that the global financial crisis sparked a renewed interest in the spillover effects of financial shocks and their policy implications among academics and policymakers alike [Kawai *et al.*, 2012; Callaghan *et al.*, 2013].

1

Another important aspect of Asia's financial linkages is related to the so-called financialization of commodity markets. This is a phenomenon characterized by a close correlation of prices between commodities and financial assets [Nissanke, 2012; Morana, 2013]. A key consequence of this financialization process is that commodity prices are determined not only by their supply and demand, but also by financial market conditions. As a result, even in the absence of close financial linkages, financial shocks can seriously affect the stability of resource-dependent economies through a variation in commodity export prices. A large variation in commodity prices can also affect the long-run economic growth of resource-dependent economies. For example, commodity price booms can slow down economic growth if it causes the Dutch disease, in which the overvaluation of real exchange rates causes deindustrialization [Corden and Neary, 1982]. Empirical evidence supports the proposition that diversification into modern manufacturing sectors is positively correlated with high income levels [Imbs and Wacziarg, 2003]. The financialization of commodity markets poses additional challenges to resource-dependent economies because the Dutch disease can be caused by exogenous events in financial markets abroad.

Finally, the recent increase in overseas workers' remittances adds a new dimension to Asia's financial linkages. The remittance has become a major source of capital inflows, which is comparable to FDI and official development assistance (ODA) in some Asian countries [Barajas *et al.*, 2009; Driffeld and Jones, 2013]. There is a growing body of literature on the economic effect of remittances (see the survey in Chapter 4 by Yuan, Inoue, and Hamori in this volume). In theory, remittance inflows can be either a blessing or a curse. On the one hand, remittance inflows can accelerate economic growth by stimulating consumption and investment. On the other hand, volatile remittance inflows can be a source of macroeconomic instability. Moreover, the recipient families' dependence on remittance inflows can discourage their labor market participation and, thus, decelerate the country's economic growth. The effect of remittance inflows is likely to differ depending on a particular country context and, thus, the accumulation of empirical evidence is essential to draw any meaningful conclusions.

The purpose of this book is to empirically analyze the multifaceted nature of financial linkages in East Asia and to discuss the key policy challenges faced by the region's economies. Although the emphasis is placed on East Asia, some of the chapters cover a broader area of countries depending on the aim of the study. Particular areas of focus in these studies include: the evolution of cross-border financial linkages in East Asia; long-run economic consequences of remittance inflows and natural resource dependence; and policy priorities for the financial integration and management of resource-rich economies. A brief overview of the content of each chapter is provided below.

Part I: The Evolution of Cross-Border Financial Linkages in East Asia
Chapter 1, by Wang Chen and Takuji Kinkyo, is titled "Asian-Pacific economic linkages: Empirical evidence in the GVAR framework." This chapter examines the interdependence between business cycles in the Asia-Pacific region, further investigating how changes in trading relationships affect the transmission of macroeconomic shocks from the US, Japan, and China to other countries using the global vector autoregressive (GVAR) model. The main findings of the analysis can be summarized as follows. First, Asian-Pacific countries have a strong reaction to stock market shocks from the US and Japan. In particular, the stock markets in Asian countries all show closer linkages to the US stock market than to Japan. In addition, there is no evidence of a causal relationship from Japan to the US. Second, China is gradually increasing its impact on the Asia-Pacific region as the country's trade structure changes. Using the more recent trade structures, the authors find China's GDP to be more closely and significantly correlated with various Asian-Pacific regions. Third, oil price is still a common factor influencing Asian-Pacific economies. A statistically significant positive relationship exists between oil prices and the inflation rate, indicating that oil price change is a source of macroeconomic fluctuations.

Chapter 2, by Takashi Miyazaki and Shigeyuki Hamori, is titled "Linkages among East Asian stock markets, US financial market stress, and gold." This chapter examines the effects of financial market tightness and stock market stress in the US, as well as the shocks in gold that have attracted the interest of international investors since the global financial crisis. Next, it analyzes the linkages between eight East Asian stock markets (Korea, Indonesia, Thailand, Malaysia, the Philippines, Hong Kong, Taiwan, and Singapore) and these financial variables, based on a structural vector autoregressive (SVAR) model. According to the analysis of impulse response, both financial market tightening and stock market stress in the US depress stock returns in East Asian countries, but the persistence of their effects is dissimilar. Further, shocks to gold returns significantly and instantaneously push up returns in all countries. Meanwhile, according to variance decomposition, the forecast error variance of returns in East Asian stock markets is predominantly due to own-market variance, and the contribution of other factors is minor. In Hong Kong and Singapore, however, the relative variance contributions of financial market tightness and stock returns in the US are high in comparison to other East Asian markets. In the augmented model, taking the interdependence among East Asian stock markets into consideration, regional market factors have a greater effect on some East Asian countries than US factors.

Chapter 3, by Xiao jing Cai and Shigeyuki Hamori, is titled "Business cycle volatility and hot money in emerging East Asian markets." This chapter investigates the linkages between US short-term interest rates, hot money flows, and business cycles in four emerging East Asian countries (Thailand, Malaysia, Korea, and Indonesia) from 1981:Q1 to 2014:Q1 by employing the multivariate Markov-switching intercept autoregressive heteroskedasticity vector autoregressive model and computing the impulse response functions for these three variables. The authors observe that during the stable period, speculative capital produces an economic boom in Thailand, Malaysia, and Indonesia, while damaging Korea's economy. Furthermore, during the turmoil period, all selected countries suffer from low economic growth. Additionally, we confirm that the inflow of hot money increases in all four countries during the stable period as the US short-term interest rate decreases, and that it decreases during the crisis period as the US short-term interest rate increases gradually. The findings provide valuable insights for policymakers in the emerging East Asian countries to formulate the measures necessary for reducing the risk of economic instability arising from hot money flows.

Part II: Long-Run Economic Consequences of Remittance Inflows and Natural Resource Dependence
Chapter 4, by Nannan Yuan, Takeshi Inoue, and Shigeyuki Hamori, is titled "Dynamic impacts of remittances on economic growth in Asia: Evidence from the dynamic heterogeneous panel." The amount of migrants' remittances has increased year after year since the 1980s, and has grown significantly and enhanced the importance of external sources of finance for economic growth, especially since the early 2000s. Against the background of surges in this capital flow, an increasing number of empirical studies have analyzed whether and how remittances affect economic growth in remittance-receiving countries, though results have been inconclusive and contradictory. This chapter reinvestigates the conflicting findings concerning the remittances-growth nexus in the literature. Employing the pooled mean group (PMG) estimation approach, we examine the dynamic impacts of remittances on economic growth in Asia. Compared to other dynamic panel econometric techniques, the PMG estimator's main advantage is that it allows long-run coefficients to be homogenous and short-run coefficients, speeds of adjustment, and error variances to be heterogeneous across countries. Results, which span 16 Asian countries over the period from 1985 to 2011, show that remittances have positive and significant long-run impacts on economic growth with diminishing marginal effect. Positive impacts depend on trade openness and decrease with increasing trade openness.

Chapter 5, by Takeshi Inoue and Shigeyuki Hamori, is titled "Effects of remittances on poverty reduction in Asia." Developing countries have significantly reduced extreme poverty during the last two decades. This was mainly realized through rapid economic growth and an accompanying poverty reduction in Asia. Therefore, Asia has attracted attention as a region of growth and poverty reduction among developing countries. Recently, Asia has also gained recognition as a region comprising countries that are the top recipients of remittances. The regional breakdown indicates that South Asia and East Asia Pacific have received the largest amount of official remittances since the mid-2000s. This chapter empirically examines the impact of remittances on poverty reduction in Asia. Using unbalanced panel data for 18 Asian countries from 1980 to 2012, we estimate the models in which the poverty headcount ratio is explained by remittances and certain control variables. The empirical results indicate that remittance inflows have a positive, statistically significant effect on poverty reduction. This evidence is robust to changes in the measures of financial development and education levels. Moreover, with regard to control variables, it was found that per capita GDP and the primary or secondary school enrollment ratio improve the poverty ratio, whereas trade openness worsens poverty conditions.

Chapter 6, by Kazue Demachi and Takuji Kinkyo, is titled "Financial development and growth in resource-rich countries." This chapter empirically evaluates the effects of financial development on economic growth in countries that are rich in natural resources. The unique contribution of this study is the explicit distinction between the case of the resource dependent and that of the resource abundant. The authors use a panel data consisting of 140 countries (at maximum) and 5 periods (25 years) from 1982 to 2006 to perform dynamic panel analysis. The results using the system generalized method of moments (GMM) show that the growth-promoting effect of financial development is weaker in resource-dependent countries, but that is not the case in resource-abundant countries. This finding suggests the importance of distinguishing between resource dependence and resource abundance when evaluating the problems associated with natural resources, and that the problems seen in resource-rich countries, often categorized as the "resource curse," play a role in disturbing the sound functioning of financial mechanisms, and this, in turn, hampers economic growth.

Part III: Policy Priorities for the Financial Integration and Management of Resource-Rich Economies
Chapter 7, by Wang Chen and Takuji Kinkyo, is titled "Spillovers of financial stress shocks: Evidence and policy implications." This chapter examines the cross-border spillovers of US financial stress shocks on Asian stock markets. The estimation procedure involves two steps. First,

a vector autoregression (VAR) is estimated to identify structural shocks. Next, ordinary least squares (OLS) regressions are estimated to evaluate the impact of the identified structural shocks on stock prices in seven Asian economies (Japan, China, Hong Kong, Taiwan, Korea, Singapore, and India). The empirical results indicate that the US financial stress shock has a statistically significant cross-border spillover effect on Asian stock prices. The impact on Asian stock prices of the US financial stress shock is more persistent than that of the US real activity shock. By contrast, the US monetary policy shock has little direct spillover effect on Asian stock prices, indicating the possibility that monetary policy shock is transmitted indirectly through financial stress shock. Key policy implications derived from the analysis are two-fold. First, Asian countries should cooperate closely to address major loopholes in financial regulations. Second, Asia's advanced countries can share their experiences with less developed countries and develop guidelines for an adequate sequencing of reforms.

Chapter 8, by Kazue Demachi and Takuji Kinkyo, is titled "Challenges to macroeconomic management in resource-rich developing economies." This chapter reviews and discusses the issues and stylized facts of resource revenue management and macroeconomic stabilization in resource-rich developing countries. Macroeconomic stabilization through the management of natural resources and the revenue derived from it is a perplexing task for a low-income country with weak institutions. Macroeconomic operations in those countries need to focus on (1) buffering the government budget and domestic economy from the shocks from international price volatility and (2) the sustainable management of natural resource revenue and the achievement of equality between generations. The international community is strengthening its involvement in supporting macroeconomic management in resource-rich developing countries. However, the authors point out that several tasks remain to be addressed. In particular, weak government capacity and poor institutional quality can be serious constraints when resource revenues are used for current investment rather than saved for future consumption. Although there are some successful cases in which resource revenues are wisely used for investment without jeopardizing revenue sustainability, success depends largely on the government capacity and institutional quality of the country. Resource-rich countries are required to establish rules and systems for sound resource management and economic diversification to avoid repeating the failures of past resource-rich countries.

Chapter 9, by Satoshi Shimizu, is titled "Policies and prospects of ASEAN financial integration." This chapter examines the challenges faced by ASEAN countries as they move towards regional financial integration. ASEAN countries are moving towards increasing economic integration in the run-up to the establishment of the ASEAN Economic Community at the end of 2015. However, regional financial integration has moved forward more slowly than integration at the real economic level. Efforts to move towards regional financial integration are centering primarily on the liberalization of financial services and capital transactions, the development of settlement systems, and the development and integration of capital markets. Given that there is a wide variation in the type of financial systems and the level of development across the ASEAN, the adjustment of national interests within the region and support for less developed countries will therefore be important priorities. To minimize the risks of intraregional financial integration, sound macro-level policy management and the development of domestic financial and capital markets, as well as the creation of crisis management systems, must be treated as prerequisites for the liberalization of capital transactions. The author argues that the most important priority in the immediate future will be to raise the standard of financial systems in each country. This will facilitate intraregional financial integration and ensure that markets are ready to absorb capital flows from outside of the region.

References

Ando, M. and Kimura, F. (2005). The Formation of International Production and Distribution Networks in East Asia. In: Ito, T. and Rose, A.K. (eds.). *International Trade in East Asia*. NBER-East Asia Seminar on Economics, 14, Chicago: University of Chicago Press, pp. 177–216.

Barajas, A., Chami, R., Fullenkamp, C., Gapen, M., and Montiel, P. (2009). Do Workers' Remittances Promote Economic Growth? IMF Working Paper WP/09/153.

Callaghan, M., Ghate, C., Pickford, S., and Rathinam, F.X. (eds.). *Global Cooperation Among G20 Countries*. New Delhi: Springer.

Corden, W.M. and Neary, J.P. (1982). Booming Sector and Deindustrialization in a Small Open Economy. *Economic Journal*, 92, pp. 825–848.

Driffield, N. and Jones, C. (2013). Impact of FDI, ODA and Migrant Remittances on Economic Growth in Developing Countries: A Systems Approach. *European Journal of Development Research*, 25, pp. 173–196.

Gill, I. and Kharas, H. (2007).*An East Asian Renaissance: Ideas for Economic Growth.* Washington DC: World Bank.

Imbs, J. and Wacziarg, R. (2003). Stages of Diversification *American Economic Review*, 93(1), pp. 63–86.

Kawai, M., Lamberte, M.B., and Park, Y.C. (2012).*The Global Financial Crisis and Asia.* Oxford: Oxford University Press.

Kinkyo, T. and Hamori, S. (2014). Exchange Rate Flexibility and the Integration of the Securities Market in East Asia. *Journal of Reviews on Global Economics*, 3, pp. 293–309.

Morana, C. (2013). Oil Price Dynamics, Macro-Finance Interactions and the Role of Financial Speculations. *Journal of Banking & Finance*, 37, pp. 206–226.

Nissanke, M. (2012). Commodity Market Linkages in the Global Financial Crisis: Excess Volatility and Development Impacts. *Journal of Development Studies*, 48, pp. 732–750.

Prasad, E.S. and Rajan, R.G. (2008). A Pragmatic Approach to Capital Account Liberalization. *Journal of Economic Perspectives*, 22, pp. 149–172.

Part I

The Evolution of Cross-Border
Financial Linkages in East Asia

Chapter 1

Asian-Pacific Economic Linkages: Empirical Evidence in the GVAR Framework

Wang Chen

Graduate School of Economics, Kobe University

2-1, Rokkodai, Nada-Ku, Kobe 657-8501, Japan

Email: tinou3776@yahoo.co.jp

Takuji Kinkyo

Faculty of Economics, Kobe University

2-1, Rokkodai, Nada-Ku, Kobe 657-8501, Japan

Email: kinkyo@econ.kobe-u.ac.jp

1.1 Introduction

The integration of the global capital market has been a remarkable phenomenon of the last several decades. That market is now sufficiently large and integrated to place tighter constraints than before on the conduct of macroeconomic policies, especially under fixed exchange rate regimes [Goldstein and Mussa, 1993]. As a result of real economic and financial linkages, it has become more difficult for any country with close global linkages to escape the spillover of economic shocks originating abroad [Edwards, 2011; Berman and Martin, 2012; Bacchetta and van Wincoop, 2013]. At the same time, economic linkage within the Asian-Pacific region has also progressed at an impressive speed. For example, the Asian-Pacific region is now the world's largest and most dynamic in terms of combined Gross Domestic Product (GDP), and the Asia-Pacific Economic Cooperation (APEC) includes several of the world's biggest existing markets. In particular, China is a member of the APEC and is the world's largest trading power with a total international trade value of US$3.87 trillion in 2012. Dreger and Zhang [2014] find that Chinese economic development affects GDP growth and inflation in the advanced countries.

A large body of literature investigates global linkages using a variety of empirical methods. Asian-Pacific economic linkages have attracted considerable attention among previous studies as the Asian-Pacific region has begun to play a more and more important role in the worldwide economy. Traditionally, empirical studies on cross-country linkages focus on the spillover effects of macroeconomic shocks (e.g., monetary shock, real activity shock, inflationary shock). Chinn and Frankel [1995], adopting the cointegration test, conclude that the real interest rate parity holds for the Pacific regions. These researchers further indicated that Hong Kong, Malaysia and Taiwan are linked with both the US and Japan, while only Singapore is solely linked with the US. Auer and Mehrotra [2014] present evidence that co-movement of inflation has existed in the Asian-Pacific region for the past three decades. Miyajima *et al.* [2014] adopt a PVAR approach to examine the effect of the term premium in US treasuries on Asian economies, suggesting that a one percentage point increase in the US 10-year term premium leads to approximately 0.6 of a percentage point increase in Asian domestic long-term bond yields within three months of the shock.

Another branch of the global linkage literature is concerned with stock market linkages in emerging Asian-Pacific markets. Park [2010] finds a strong co-movement between Asian markets. In particular, countries with more developed financial systems (i.e., Japan, Singapore, and Hong Kong) exhibited stronger linkages to the rest of the Asian markets. Srinivasan and Kalaivani [2013] employ the cointegration test to examine the dynamic linkages in emerging Asian-Pacific markets, supporting the argument that there exists a common force that brings these stock markets together in the long run. Due to limitations of empirical methodology, known as the "curse of dimensionality", a large body of literature has investigated only the spillover effects in countries of interest based on limited information. To examine economic linkages in the Asian-Pacific region in a broader, more multilateral context, a more comprehensive empirical model would be needed. Because the limited number of variables is a drawback for studying cross-country spillover effects, where long time series and many variables are essential, there have been two approaches recently introduced to reduce dimension: the Factor Augmented VAR (FAVAR) and the Global VAR (GVAR).

The FAVAR model was originally used by Bernanke *et al.* [2005] to identify a US monetary policy shock and examine its macroeconomic impacts. The traditional VAR can suffer from an identification problem arising from omitted variable biases, while the FAVAR can circumvent this problem by exploiting the rich information contained in common factors extracted from a large set of economic variables. An example of the FAVAR approach used to study international transmission mechanisms is in the work of Benkovskis *et al.* [2011]. Using the FAVAR, they find that an unexpected increase in the euro area interest rate results in a contraction of economic activity in the Czech Republic, Poland and Hungary, concluding that the foreign demand and interest rate effects dominate the reaction of real economic activity variables, while the exchange rate effect is important for price reactions, leading to higher export and import deflators.

The GVAR model was developed and expanded by Pesaran *et al.* [2004], Pesaran and Smith [2006], Garratt *et al.* [2006], and di Mauro and Pesaran [2013]. An important feature of the GVAR approach is that it combines individual error-correcting models for a selected set of countries or regions and estimates them in one model by weekly exogenous assumption on foreign-specific variables. The foreign-specific variables are computed as weighted averages of the corresponding domestic variables of all countries. Most previous GVAR studies of international linkages use trade weights. It is worth noting that the trade weights can also be set to time-varying trade weights, allowing research to consider how changes in trade patterns might have affected the international transmission mechanisms. This option is another advantage of GVAR compared with the FAVAR model.

In this chapter, we aim to examine the interdependence between the business cycles in Asian-Pacific region, further investigating how changes in the trading relationships affect the transmission of macroeconomic shocks from the US, Japan, and China to other countries in the context of the GVAR model. The effect of greater trade integration on business cycle synchronization is ambiguous. Some reports argue that greater trade integration should lead to stronger spillovers of demand shocks to other countries. Choe [2001] focuses on the business cycles between 10 East Asian countries, finding that economic fluctuations tend to be more synchronized within the region as trade interdependence among them deepens. However, Imbs [2000] shows that while the rise in trade between 1963 and 1990 caused a small increase in synchronization, it has been more than offset by increased specialization, which may lead to lower synchronization. Similarly, Crosby [2003] examines GDP linkages in 13 Asian pacific countries, finding that trade does not explain correlations in the Asian-Pacific region.

The rest of the chapter is structured as follows. Section 1.2 outlines the GVAR model and the data used in the empirical application, while Section 1.3 analyses the empirical results. Finally, Section 1.4 presents the conclusions.

1.2 Methodology and Data

The GVAR model is based on individual VARX*s for $N+1$ countries. These countries are indexed by $i = 0,1,2,\cdots,N$, adopting country 0 as the reference country. For each country, the VARX* model includes domestic variables and weakly exogenous country-specific foreign variables. The assumption of weak exogeneity of the country-specific foreign variables implies that the foreign variables are long-run forcing for the domestic variables, but domestic variables do not affect foreign variables in the long term. In the VARX*(1,1) specification

$$\mathbf{x}_{it} = \mathbf{a}_{io} + \mathbf{a}_{i1}t + \boldsymbol{\Phi}_i \mathbf{x}_{i,t-1} + \boldsymbol{\Lambda}_{i0}\mathbf{x}^*_{it} + \boldsymbol{\Lambda}_{i1}\mathbf{x}^*_{i,t-1} + \mathbf{u}_{it} \tag{1.1}$$

$\mathbf{x}_{it}$ denotes the $k_i \times 1$ vector of country specific variables, and $\mathbf{x}^*_{it}$ denotes the $k_i^* \times 1$ vector of foreign variables, constructed by weights relevant for the specific country. The system might be extended by common factors representing global variables (e.g., oil prices). Further, $\boldsymbol{\Phi}_i$ is a $k_i \times k_i$ matrix of lagged coefficients, and $\boldsymbol{\Lambda}_{i0}$ and $\boldsymbol{\Lambda}_{i1}$ are $k_i \times k_i^*$ matrices associated with the coefficients of the foreign variables that can enter contemporaneous and lagged form; $\mathbf{a}_{io}$ denotes a constant, t denotes a linear trend, and $\mathbf{u}_{it}$ is a process with no serial correlation but with weak dependency over cross sections.

The foreign variables $\mathbf{x}^*_{it}$ in a country VARX* are constructed as weighted averages of other countries' variables. To be specific, the set of foreign specific variables for the i th country is

$$\mathbf{x}^*_{it} = \sum_{j=0}^{N} w_{ij} \mathbf{x}_{jt}$$

where w_{ij} denotes the weights that reflect the trade share of country j in the trade of country i. The weights are predetermined and satisfy the conditions $w_{ii} = 0$ and $\sum_{j=0}^{N} w_{ij} = 1$. We also use the time-varying trade weight to investigate how the changes in trade relationships affect the transmission of macroeconomic shocks. This is important because, as emerging markets have developed at an astonishing speed over the last decade, world trade relationships have changed over time. Each VARX* is estimated separately to solve the problem of the curse of dimensionality. Estimation is performed by transforming the VARX* model into a VECMX* model. The error-correction form VECMX* of Eq. (1.1) can be written as

$$\Delta\mathbf{x}_{it} = \mathbf{a}_{io} + \mathbf{a}_{i1}t - \left(\mathbf{I}_{k_i} - \boldsymbol{\Phi}_i\right)\mathbf{x}_{i,t-1} + (\boldsymbol{\Lambda}_{i0} + \boldsymbol{\Lambda}_{i1})\mathbf{x}^*_{i,t-1} + \boldsymbol{\Lambda}_{i0}\Delta\mathbf{x}^*_{it} + \mathbf{u}_{it}$$

$$\tag{1.2}$$

Using $\mathbf{z}_{it} = (\mathbf{x}'_{it}, \mathbf{x}^{*'}_{it})'$, Eq.(1.2) can be transformed to

$$\Delta\mathbf{x}_{it} = \mathbf{c}_{i0} - \boldsymbol{\alpha}_i\boldsymbol{\beta}'_i[\mathbf{z}_{i,t-1} - \boldsymbol{\gamma}_i(t-1)] + \boldsymbol{\Lambda}_{i0}\Delta\mathbf{x}^*_{it} + \mathbf{u}_{it} \qquad (1.3)$$

where $\boldsymbol{\alpha}_i$ is a $k_i \times r_i$ matrix with the speed of adjustment coefficients, and $\boldsymbol{\beta}_i$ is a $(k_i + k_i^*) \times r_i$ matrix with the cointegration vectors. The rank of both $\boldsymbol{\alpha}_i$ and $\boldsymbol{\beta}_i$ is r_i. The error-correction terms of Eq. (1.3) can be rewritten as

$$\boldsymbol{\beta}'_i(\mathbf{z}_{it} - \boldsymbol{\gamma}_i t) = \boldsymbol{\beta}'_{ix}\mathbf{x}_{it} + \boldsymbol{\beta}'_{ix^*}\mathbf{x}^*_{ix} - (\boldsymbol{\beta}'_i\boldsymbol{\gamma}_i)t \qquad (1.4)$$

Eq. (1.4) allows the possibility of cointegration both within $\mathbf{x}_{it}$ and across $\mathbf{x}_{it}$ and $\mathbf{x}^*_{it}$, and consequently across $\mathbf{x}_{it}$ and $\mathbf{x}_{jt}$ for $i \neq j$. The estimation is based on reduced rank regression and provides estimates of the rank orders of the VECMX* model r_i, the speed of adjustment coefficient $\boldsymbol{\alpha}_i$ and the cointegration vector $\boldsymbol{\beta}_i$ for each country. Conditional on the estimate above for $\boldsymbol{\beta}_i$, the remaining parameters of the VECMX* model for country i are then estimated using the OLS estimator.

Once the VECMX* model is estimated for each country, the GVAR model is solved simultaneously for all the countries for all the endogenous variables in the global system as follows:

First, use $\mathbf{z}_{it} = (\mathbf{x}'_{it}, \mathbf{x}^{*'}_{it})'$ to rewrite Eq. (1.1) as

$$\mathbf{A}_{i0}\mathbf{z}_{it} = \mathbf{a}_{i0} + \mathbf{a}_{i1}\mathbf{t} + \mathbf{A}_{i1}\mathbf{z}_{i,t-1} + \mathbf{u}_{it} \qquad (1.5)$$

where $\mathbf{A}_{i0} = (\mathbf{I}_{k_i} - \boldsymbol{\Lambda}_{i0})$, $\mathbf{A}_{i1} = (\boldsymbol{\Phi}_i, \boldsymbol{\Lambda}_{i1})$

Second, use $\mathbf{z}_{it} = \mathbf{W}_i\mathbf{x}_t$, where $\mathbf{x}_t = (\mathbf{x}'_{0t}, \mathbf{x}'_{1t}, \cdots \mathbf{x}'_{Nt})'$ is a $k \times 1$ vector of endogenous variables and $\mathbf{W}_i$ is a $(k_i + k_i^*) \times k$ link matrix. $\mathbf{W}_i$ is constructed from the country-specific trade weight w_{ij}. Use the identity above to rewrite Eq. (1.5) as

$$\mathbf{A}_{i0}\mathbf{W}_i\mathbf{x}_t = \mathbf{a}_{i0} + \mathbf{a}_{i1}\mathbf{t} + \mathbf{A}_{i1}\mathbf{W}_i\mathbf{x}_{t-1} + \mathbf{u}_{it} \qquad (1.6)$$

By stacking the individual models

$$\mathbf{G}_0\mathbf{x}_t = \mathbf{a}_0 + \mathbf{a}_1\mathbf{t} + \mathbf{G}_1\mathbf{x}_{t-1} + \mathbf{u}_t \qquad (1.7)$$

where

$$
\mathbf{G}_0 = \begin{pmatrix} \mathbf{A}_{00}\mathbf{W}_0 \\ \mathbf{A}_{10}\mathbf{W}_1 \\ \vdots \\ \mathbf{A}_{N0}\mathbf{W}_N \end{pmatrix}, \ \mathbf{G}_1 = \begin{pmatrix} \mathbf{A}_{01}\mathbf{W}_0 \\ \mathbf{A}_{11}\mathbf{W}_1 \\ \vdots \\ \mathbf{A}_{N1}\mathbf{W}_N \end{pmatrix}, \ \mathbf{a}_0 = \begin{pmatrix} \mathbf{a}_{00} \\ \mathbf{a}_{10} \\ \vdots \\ \mathbf{a}_{N0} \end{pmatrix}, \ \mathbf{a}_1 = \begin{pmatrix} \mathbf{a}_{01} \\ \mathbf{a}_{11} \\ \vdots \\ \mathbf{a}_{N1} \end{pmatrix}, \ \mathbf{u}_t = \begin{pmatrix} \mathbf{u}_{0t} \\ \mathbf{u}_{1t} \\ \vdots \\ \mathbf{u}_{Nt} \end{pmatrix}
$$

The $\mathbf{G}_0$ matrix is of $k \times k$ dimension is nonsingular, and Eq. (1.7) can be solved for $\mathbf{x}_t$.

We use GVAR Toolbox (2.0) [Smith and Galesi, 2014] to specify and estimate the GVAR models. The database includes quarterly data for 33 countries from 1979Q1 to 2013Q1, including 8 of the 11 countries that originally joined the euro area (that is, Austria, Belgium, Finland, France, Germany, Italy, the Netherlands and Spain) [a]. Each country model includes six variables (real output (y_{it}), inflation (Δp_{it}), real exchange rate ($e_{it} - p_{it}$), real equity price (eq_{it}), short-term interest rate (ρ_{it}^{S}), and long-term interest rate (ρ_{it}^{L})). However, considering the limitations of the data, some country models do not contain all variables. The US model also contains oil prices, based on taking oil prices (p_t^{o}) as an endogenous determinant variable in the US model. The variables are defined as follows:

$$
y_{it} = \ln(GDP_{it} - CPI_{it}), \ p_{it} = \ln(CPI_{it}), \ eq_{it} = \ln(EQ_{it} / CPI_{it}),
$$
$$
e_{it} = \ln(E_{it}), \rho_{it}^{S} = 0.25\ln(1 + R_{it}^{S} / 100), \rho_{it}^{L} = 0.25\ln(1 + R_{it}^{L} / 100),
$$
$$
p_t^{o} = \ln(P_t^{o})
$$

where GDP_{it} =nominal Gross Domestic Product of country i during period t, in domestic currency; CPI_{it} =Consumer Price Index in country i at time t; EQ_{it} =nominal Equity Price Index; E_{it} = exchange rate of country i at time t in terms of US dollars; R_{it}^{S} = nominal short-term rate of interest per annum, in percent; R_{it}^{L} = nominal long-term rate of

---

[a] See Appendix for more information on the domestic and foreign variables included in the country-specific model.

interest per annum, in percent; and P_t^o = price of oil[b]. To incorporate the recent shift in international trade linkages, we construct the foreign-specific variables for each country using a fixed trade weight over the three years 2011Q1–2013Q1. In addition, we use the time-varying trade weight to investigate how the changes in trading relationships affect the transmission of macroeconomic shocks from the US, China, and Japan to other Asian countries.

1.3   Empirical Results

Given the simultaneous nature of the GVAR model, an informative comparative analysis of dynamics and interdependence can be drawn from the impulse response function. One possible approach to the identification of the shocks is the orthogonalized impulse response function (OIRF) analysis of Sims [1980]. The OIRF approach requires the impulse response to be computed with respect to a set of orthogonalized shocks. This assumption is difficult for the GVAR model. Even if a suitable ordering of the variables in a given country model is derived from economic theory, it is not clear how to order counties when applying the OIRF to the GVAR model. Following Pesaran *et al.* [2004], and Pesaran and Smith [2006], we adopt the generalized impulse response function (GIRF) approach, advanced in Koop *et al.* [1996] and Pesaran and Shin [1998]. It is worth noting that the GIRF approach does not seek to identify shocks according to some canonical system, so the GIRF approach cannot provide information on the reasons behind the changes. However, with the aid of GIRF, we can simulate the historical correlations of the shock of interest. The GIRF is defined as

$$GIRFs(\mathbf{x}_t; \mathbf{u}_{ilt}, n) = E(\mathbf{x}_{t+n} | \mathbf{u}_{ilt} = \sqrt{\sigma_{jj,ll}}, \mathbf{\Omega}_{t-1}) - E(\mathbf{x}_{t+n} | \mathbf{\Omega}_{t-1})$$

---

[b] The data source used in the GVAR model can be downloaded from the International Financial Statistics database, the Inter-American Development Bank Latin Macro Watch database, and the Bloomberg database. In this chapter, we directly download the dataset from the following website: https://sites.google.com/site/gvarmodelling/gvar-toolbox.

where Ω_{t-1} is the information set at time $t-1$, $\sigma_{jj,ll}$ is the diagonal element of the variance-covariance matrix Σ_u corresponding to the lth equation in the ith country, and n is the horizon. For illustrative purposes, we mainly examine the following three aspects: (1) a one standard error negative shock to US/Japan real equity prices;[c] (2) a one standard error positive shock to the US/China/Japan real GDP in the context of the time-varying trade weight; and (3) a one standard error positive shock to oil prices. The GIRFs are presented for 24 quarters. The 90% bootstrap confidence bands have been computed by simulations using 500 replications.

1.3.1 Negative shock to US/Japan real equity prices

Figures 1.1 and 1.2 shows the estimate cumulative impulse response of individual countries' equity prices to negative shocks to US and Japan equity prices. The statistically significant response indicates that the US stock market is closely linked with the stock markets of other Asian-Pacific countries. Among them, Singapore shows the most pronounced response, suggesting a strong linkage between them. Asian countries also show a statistically significant response to stock market shock from Japan, although the correlation is less strong than that with the US stock market. In addition, we do not find the stock market of the US to exhibit a statistically significant response to a real equity shock from Japan. This result is very similar to the findings of Floros [2005], which reported a unidirectional causal relationship between the US S&P 500 and the Japan Nikkei 225, indicating that the S&P 500 stock index affects the Nikkei 225 stock index, but not vice versa. Floros [2005] concludes that the US stock market plays a leading role in Asian stock markets.

1.3.2 Positive shock to US/China/Japan real GDP

To examine whether the co-movements of shocks to the US/China/Japan GDP on Asian countries have changed over time, we vary the trade weights with time: 1985, 1995, 2005, and 2012. The effect of a one

---

[c] The impact of China's equity price shocks is not examined due to the data limitation of China's equity prices.

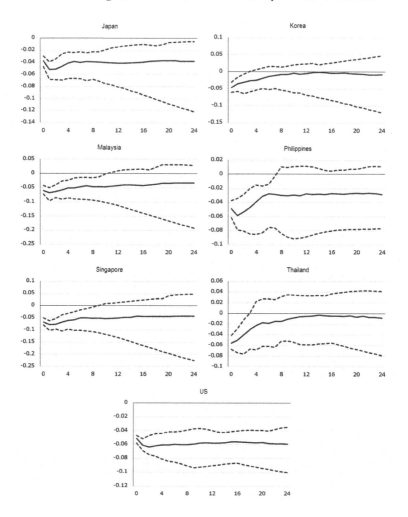

Figure 1.1. Generalized impulse responses of a one-standard-error shock (-) to US real equity prices on real equity prices across countries.

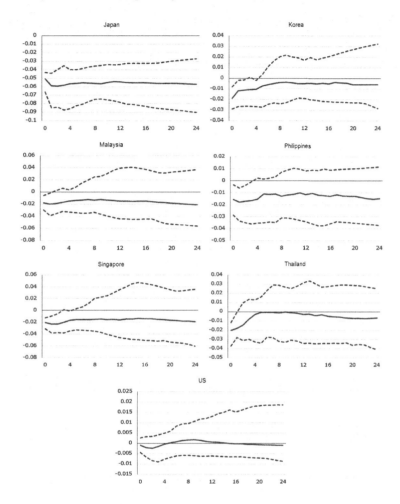

Figure 1.2. Generalized impulse responses of a one-standard-error shock (-) to Japan real equity prices on real equity prices across countries.

standard error positive shock to the US/China/Japan real GDP is compared for the different years to quantify any differences. From Figure 1.3, 1.4 and 1.5 we find a positive association between the US real GDP and each Asian country except for the Philippines. In the case of Japan, we also see similar results except for Korea. Further, we find that the correlation of the Japan GDP and other Asian-Pacific GDPs was strongest during the 1990s. In contrast, we find some evidence indicating that since the 1990s, the real activity linkages between China and other Asian-Pacific countries have significantly increased in many countries, except for Korea. This result is similar to Cesa-Bianchi *et al.* [2012], suggesting that the impact of China on Latin American economies has increased over the past two decades with deepening internationalization.

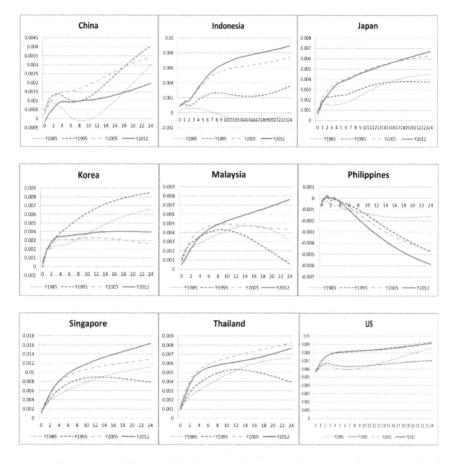

Figure 1.3. Generalized impulse responses of a one-standard-error shock to US real output on real output across countries.

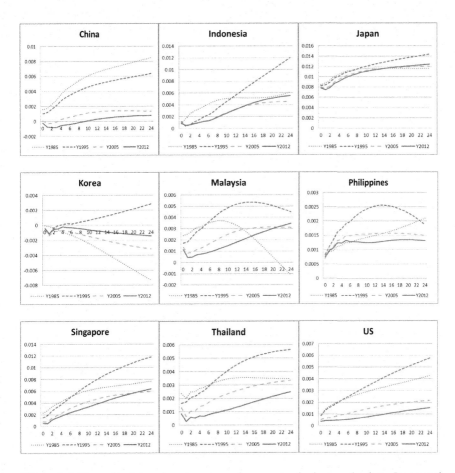

Figure 1.4. Generalized impulse responses of a one-standard-error shock to Japan real output on real output across countries.

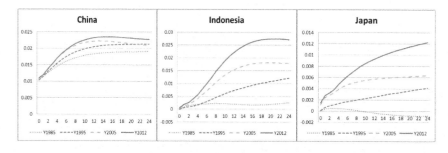

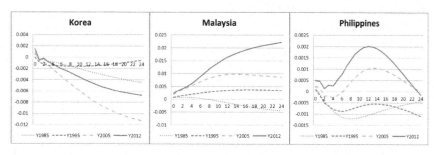

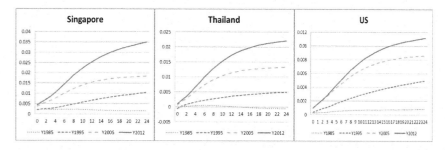

Figure 1.5. Generalized impulse responses of a one-standard-error shock to China real output on real output across countries.

1.3.3 *Positive shock to oil prices*

We also examine the effect of oil price changes on Asian-Pacific inflation. Figure 1.6 highlights a statistically significant positive relation between oil prices and inflationary pressure, except in China, where we do not find a significant relation.

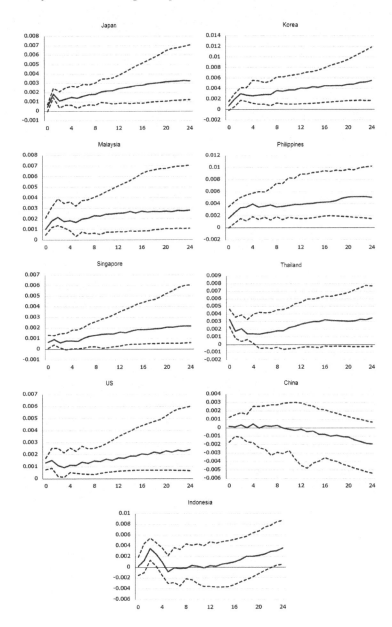

Figure 1.6. Generalized impulse responses of a one-standard-error shock to oil prices on inflation rate across countries.

1.4 Conclusions

In this chapter, we examined and evaluated the economic linkages involving the Asia-Pacific region in the context of a GVAR model. The main finding of the analysis can be summarized as follows. First, the Asian-Pacific countries have a strong reaction to stock market shocks from US and Japan. In particular, the stock markets in Asian countries all show closer linkages with the US stock market than Japan. In addition, there is no evidence of a causal relationship from Japan to the US stock markets. Second, China is gradually increasing its impact on the Asia-Pacific region as the country's trade structure changes. Using the more recent trade structures of 2005 and 2012, we find the China GDP to be more closely and significantly correlated with various Asian-Pacific regions. Third, oil price is still a common factor influencing Asian-Pacific economies. A statistically significant positive relationship exists between oil prices and inflation rate, indicating that oil price change is a source of macroeconomic fluctuations.

Appendix 1.1 Countries in the GVAR model
ARGENTINA, AUSTRALIA, AUSTRIA, BELGIUM, BRAZIL, CANADA, CHINA, CHILE, FINLAND, FRANCE, GERMANY, INDIA, INDONESIA, ITALY, JAPAN, KOREA, MALAYSIA, MEXICO, NETHERLANDS, NORWAY, NEW ZEALAND, PERU, PHILIPPINES, SOUTH AFRICA, SAUDIARABIA, SINGAPORE, SPAIN, SWEDEN, SWITZERLAND, THAILAND, TURKEY, UNITED KINGDOM, AND UNITED STATES OF AMERICA.

Appendix 1.2 Domestic and foreign variables included in the country-specific model

| Variables | All countries excluding US | | US | |
	Endogenous	Foreign	Endogenous	Foreign
Real output	y_{it}	y_{it}^*	$y_{US,t}$	$y_{US,t}^*$
Inflation	Δp_{it}	Δp_{it}^*	$\Delta p_{US,t}$	$\Delta p_{US,t}^*$
Real exchange rate	$e_{it} - p_{it}$	-	-	$e_{US,t}^* - p_{US,t}^*$
Real equity price	eq_{it}	eq_{it}^*	$eq_{US,t}$	-
Short-term interest rate	ρ_{it}^S	ρ_{it}^{*S}	$\rho_{US,t}^S$	-
Long-term interest rate	ρ_{it}^L	ρ_{it}^{*L}	$\rho_{US,t}^L$	-
Oil price	-	p_t^o	p_t^o	-

References

Auer, R. and Mehrotra, A. (2014). Trade linkages and the globalisation of inflation in Asia and the Pacific, *BIS Working Papers*, No. 447.

Bacchetta, P. and van Wincoop, E. (2013). Sudden spikes in global risk, *Journal of International Economics*, 89, pp. 511–521.

Benkovskis, K., Bessonovs, A., Feldkircher, M. and Wörz, J. (2011). The Transmission of Euro Area Monetary Shocks to the Czech Republic, Poland and Hungary: Evidence from a FAVAR Model, Focus on the European Economic Integration, pp. 8–36.

Berman, N. and Martin, P. (2012). The vulnerability of sub-Sahara Africa to the financial crisis: the case of trade, *IMF Economic Review*, 60(3), pp. 329–364.

Bernanke, B.S., Boivin, J. and Eliasz, P. (2005). Measuring the effects of monetary policy: a factor-augmented vector autoregressive (FAVAR) approach, *Quarterly Journal of Economics*, February, pp. 387–422.

Cesa-Bianchi, A., Pesaran, M.H., Rebucci, A. and Xu, T. (2012). China's emergence in the world economy and business cycles in Latin America, *Economia*, 12(2), pp. 1–75.

Chinn, M.D. and Frankel, J.A. (1995). Who drives real interest rates around the Pacific Rim: the USA or Japan? *Journal of International Money and Finance*, 14(6), pp. 801–821.

Choe, J-Il. (2001). An impact of economic integration through trade: on business cycles for 10 East Asian countries, *Journal of Asian Economics*, 12(4), pp. 569–586.

Crosby, M. (2003). Business cycle correlations in Asia-Pacific, *Economics Letters*, 80(1), pp. 35–44.

di Mauro, F. and Pesaran, M.H. (2013) *The GVAR Handbook: Structure and Applications of a Macro Model of the Global Economy for Policy Analysis*, (Oxford University Press, Oxford).

Dreger, C. and Zhang, Y. (2014). Does the economic integration of China affect growth and inflation in industrial countries? *Economic Modelling*, 38, pp. 184–189.

Edwards, S. (2011). Exchange rates in emerging countries: eleven empirical regularities from Latin America and East Asia, *National Bureau of Economic Research (NBER) Working Papers*, 17074.

Floros, C. (2005). Price linkages between the US, Japan and UK stock markets, *Financial Markets and Portfolio Management*, 19(2), pp. 169–178.

Garratt, T., Lee, K., Pesaran, M.H. and Shin, Y. (2006) *Global and National Macroeconometric Modelling: A Long Run Structural Approach*, (Oxford University Press, Oxford).

Goldstein, M. and Mussa, M. (1993). The Integration of World Capital Markets, *International Monetary Fund (IMF) Working Papers*, pp. 93–95.

Imbs, J. (2000). Sectors and the OECD Business Cycle, *CEPR Discussion Paper*, No. 2473.

Koop, G., Pesaran, M.H. and Potter, S.M. (1996). Impulse response analysis in nonlinear multivariate models, *Journal of Econometrics*, 74(1), pp. 119–147.

Miyajima, K., Mohanty, M.S. and Yetman, J. (2014). Spillovers of US unconventional monetary policy to Asia: the role of long-term interest, *BIS Working Papers*, No 478.

Park, J.W. (2010). Comovement of Asian Stock Markets and the U.S. Influence, *Global Economy and Finance Journal*, 3(2), pp. 76–88.

Pesaran, M.H., Schuermann, T. and Weiner, S.M. (2004). Modeling regional interdependencies using a global error-correcting macroeconometric model, *Journal of Business & Economic Statistics*, 22(2), pp. 129–162.

Pesaran, M.H. and Shin, Y. (1998). Generalized impulse response analysis in linear multivariate models, *Economics Letters*, 58(1), pp. 17–29.

Pesaran, M.H. and Smith, R. (2006). Macroeconometric modelling with a global perspective, *Manchester School*, 74, pp. 24–49.

Sims, C.A. (1980). Macroeconomics and Reality, *Econometrica*, 48, pp. 1–48.

Smith, L.V. and Galesi, A. (2014) *GVAR toolbox 2.0.* https://sites.google.com/site/gvarmodelling/gvar–toolbox.

Srinivasan, P. and Kalaivani, M. (2013). Stock Market Linkages in Emerging Asia-Pacific Markets, *MPRA Paper*, No. 45871.

Chapter 2

Linkages among East Asian Stock Markets, US Financial Markets Stress, and Gold

Takashi Miyazaki

Japan Center for Economic Research

Nikkei Bldg. 11F, 1-3-7 Otemachi,

Chiyoda-Ku, Tokyo 100-8066, Japan

Email: most_likelihood@yahoo.co.jp

Shigeyuki Hamori

Faculty of Economics, Kobe University

2-1, Rokkodai, Nada-Ku, Kobe 657-8501, Japan

Email: hamori@econ.kobe-u.ac.jp

2.1 Introduction

There are many existing studies on the international transmission of shocks in stock markets. As will be mentioned in the literature review of Section 2.2 below, much of the existing research regarding the international transmission of shocks in stock markets suggests that the

US financial market still possesses a dominant influence over external countries' stock markets. The recent severe global financial crisis propagated worldwide from the US as the originator to other economies, including emerging markets.

The aim in this chapter is to quantify how financial market tightness and stock market stress in the US, and in gold, affect stock markets in East Asian countries (i.e., Korea, Indonesia, Thailand, Malaysia, the Philippines, Hong Kong, Taiwan, and Singapore), based on a structural vector autoregressive (VAR) model. Specifically, we examine the impact and contribution of (i) shocks (innovations) to high volatility regime probability in the US stock market; (ii) shock (innovation) to financial market tightness in the US; and (iii) shock (innovation) in gold return, to East Asian stock markets. Additionally, we incorporate regional factors of East Asian stock markets into the model, and assess their impact on individual markets.

We capture the upsurge of stock market stress in the US as a shock to the smoothed state probability for the high volatility regime, derived from a simple Markov-switching model. To our knowledge, there is no previous study introducing state probabilities obtained from a Markov-switching model into a system of structural VAR.

Further, in recent years, literature pointing out the progress of the financialization of commodities has increased [i.e., Domanski and Heath, 2007; Miyazaki and Hamori, 2014; Tang and Xiong, 2012]. Although the gold price rose persistently from the latter half of 2005 and peaked at about 1900 US dollars/oz, the price declined to about 1,300 US dollars/oz as of the end of July 2014. In particular, gold has attracted investors' interest as an alternative investment to flight to quality, or to hedge against stock market crashes since the recent global financial crisis. In response to this fact, we introduce gold return into our structural VAR system. To date, academic research dealing with the interdependence between gold and stock returns is comparatively rare[a]. Our analysis also helps to correct this discrepancy.

---

[a] Miyazaki *et al.* [2012] analyze the interdependence among returns of gold, stock, bond, and exchange rate by employing the Asymmetric Dynamic Conditional Correlation (A-

Our empirical results demonstrate that financial market tightening and an upsurge of stock market stress in the US exert a significant negative impact on East Asian stock markets. On the one hand, financial market tightening sharply and immediately depresses stock returns; on the other hand, stock market stress moderately dampens these returns for some time, with a short lag. In addition, we obtain evidence that countries with developed stock markets are more influenced by the US market, which is consistent with intuition. Meanwhile, although gold return is positively and significantly linked to East Asian stock returns, its contribution to the error variance of returns is substantially limited.

The structure of this chapter is organized as follows. In the next section, we review previous studies related to our analysis. Section 2.3 describes the framework of empirical analysis and constructs variables introduced in later section. In section 2.4, we present data used, and Section 2.5 provides the empirical results. Lastly, section 2.6 concludes.

2.2 Literature Review

As mentioned in the Introduction, many previous studies have accumulated focusing on the international transmission of shocks in stock markets. In this section, we primarily review existing research examining the transmission of shocks in advanced markets such as the US to emerging markets such as Asian countries.

Eun and Shim [1989] and Hamao *et al.* [1990] are pioneering works that analyze the international transmission mechanisms of stock return and volatility. Eun and Shim [1989] studied the international transmission mechanism of nine stock market returns, namely, Australia, Canada, France, Germany, Hong Kong, Japan, Switzerland, the UK, and the US, based on VAR modeling. Their results show that, on the one hand, shocks originating in the US transmit quickly; on the other hand, other countries' shock does not explain fluctuations in the US market. Hamao *et al.* [1990] examined the spillover effects of volatility among

DCC) model. Miyazaki and Hamori [2013] perform statistical tests for causality between gold and stock for both returns and volatilities.

New York, London, and Japan, based on a GARCH type model. They confirm that there exists volatility in spillover effects from New York to London and Japan, and from London to Japan, over their sample period, which includes Black Monday.

Masih and Masih [1997] and Liu *et al.* [1998] are earlier papers that assess the interdependence between developed countries and emerging Asian markets. Masih and Masih [1997] examined the dynamic pattern of linkages between new industrialized economies, NIEs (Taiwan, Korea, Singapore, and Hong Kong), and industrialized economies (the US, the UK, Japan, and Germany). They show that industrialized economies and Hong Kong play a leading role in the fluctuation of NIEs, and reveal that Taiwan and Singapore, especially Taiwan, are vulnerable to shocks stemming from industrialized economies in the short run[b]. Liu *et al.* [1998] analyzed transmission mechanisms in stock markets for the US, Japan, Hong Kong, Singapore, Taiwan, and Thailand. They showed that (1) the interdependence has increased since the 1987 stock market crash; (2) the US market possesses a dominant influence over Asian markets; (3) Japan and Singapore have significant and persistent impacts on other Asian markets; and 4) Taiwan and Thailand are not efficient in terms of information processing.

Cha and Oh [2000] also analyzed the relationships between stock markets in advanced countries (i.e., the US and Japan) and four Asian emerging economies (Hong Kong, Korea, Singapore, and Taiwan). Their results suggested that the linkages among these countries started to strengthen after Black Monday, as in Hamao *et al.* [1990], and had intensified significantly since the Asian currency crisis in July 1997.

From the perspective of capital market integration, Phylaktis [1999] analyzed financial influences from the US and Japan on the Pacific Basin countries, taking up money markets. Her analysis showed that these countries are more closely linked to Japan than to the US. Looking at almost the same set of samples, Phylaktis and Ravazzolo [2005]

---

[b] Masih and Masih [2001] extends the analysis of Masih and Masih [1997]. Refer also to Sheng and Tu [2000], Darrat and Zhong [2002], Bessler and Yang [2003], and Yang *et al.* [2003, 2006] for the application of cointegration techniques to the analysis of causal linkages in the long run.

examined the stock market linkages among the US, Japan, and Pacific Basin countries. According to their results, although deregulation of restrictions on foreign investment in the 1980s had not sufficiently attracted investors' interest and other factors influenced decisions on diversification, by the 1990s, the interrelationships among international markets had strengthened.

Gebka and Serwa [2006] investigated the structural change (i.e., the number of regimes of causal pattern) in spillovers from the US to eight East Asian capital markets. Their analysis revealed that the linkages between the US and Asian markets follow two regimes, and that spillover effects are strengthened in crisis regimes. Miyakoshi [2003] analyzed the spillover effects of return and volatility from the US to Japan and to seven Asian economies. His results suggested that (1) the US is only important for returns in Asian markets; (2) Japan is more influential than the US regarding volatility in Asia; and (3) there is a feedback effect between Japan and Asian markets[c].

Studies based on the Dynamic Conditional Correlation (DCC) model developed by Engle [2002] are given by Naoui *et al.* [2010] and Hyde *et al.* [2008]. Naoui *et al.* [2010] applied the DCC model to an analysis of financial contagion in the recent crisis caused by the subprime mortgage problem. They examined the interdependence between the US and other developed and emerging economies including Asia, and find that there exist two country groups, which either have or do not have high correlations with the US. Hyde *et al.* [2008] investigated the stock market linkages between Asia-Pacific, the EU, and the US, using an asymmetric generalized dynamic conditional correlation (AG-DCC) model. They confirmed the significant asymmetry in correlations among these markets, thereby reinforcing the conventional view that correlations increase in response to negative news or shocks (e.g., financial turmoil).

There are also plenty of previous works investigating the interdependence among Asian markets, particularly in the context of

---

[c] For volatility transmission, Chuang *et al.* [2007] also show that there is significant influence from Japan to Asian markets, centered upon NIEs, although they do not include the US in the sample.

contagion effects in Asian currency crises [i.e., Billio and Pelizzon, 2003; Forbes and Rigobon, 2002; Chiang *et al.*, 2007; Corsetti *et al.*, 2005; Sander and Kleimeier, 2003][d]. In recent years, Fujiwara and Takahashi [2012] analyze the interactions between Asian financial markets and the real economy, using a spillover index developed by Diebold and Yilmaz [2009]. They emphasize the importance of common global shocks. In addition, they show that the US plays a dominant role in Asian stock and bond market fluctuations, and that China emerges as a source of fluctuation in the real economy.

In terms of methodology and research interest, Tytell *et al.* [2009] and, Park and Mercado [2013] are closely related to the present study. These works investigate the transmission mechanisms of financial stress from advanced countries to emerging markets in financial crises. They present the common empirical result that there exist transmission mechanisms from the former to the latter markets.

As reviewed above, most of the existing literature provides evidence that the contribution of the US to foreign markets is still important for the international transmission of shocks in financial markets. In the following section, we perform an empirical analysis focusing on the transmission mechanism of shocks originating in the US stock and financial markets to East Asian stock markets.

2.3 Framework of Empirical Analysis

We analyze the effects of change in stock market regime and financial market tightening in the US on East Asian stock markets, by employing impulse response and variance decomposition derived from a structural VAR model. To this end, we need to construct the variables representing stock market regime and financial market tightness in the US. The basic framework of empirical analysis in this chapter is as follows.

First, we estimate a two-regime Markov-switching first-order autoregressive (MS(2)-AR(1)) model for S&P500 index return, and

---

[d] Yiu *et al.* [2010] investigate the contagion among Asian markets in the recent global financial crisis.

deliver the smoothed state probability for a high volatility regime. This smoothed state probability is used as an endogenous variable in the following structural VAR estimation. Next, we extract risk factors in financial markets from the group of TED spread, term spread, default premium, and VIX, by applying principal component analysis. The first principal component, which is considered as a variable representing financial market stress or tightness, is introduced as an endogenous variable in our structural VAR. Finally, we estimate a structural VAR model including the variables explained above and returns of S&P500 index, each East Asian stock market, and gold, and derive impulse response and forecast error variance decomposition of East Asian stock returns. Note that for impulse response analysis, we employ a generalized impulse response that does not depend on the order of variables, since we do not have any prior information on the variables' ordering [Koop *et al.*, 1996; Pesaran and Shin, 1998][e].

To begin with, we estimate a simple Markov-switching model to construct variables of stock market stress and uncertainty in the US. To identify the regime in the US stock market, we estimate a simple Markov-switching first-order autoregressive model with two regimes for S&P500 index returns:

$$ y_t = \alpha_{S_t} + \beta_{S_t} y_{t-1} + \varepsilon_t, \quad t = 1, \cdots, T, \quad \varepsilon_t \sim NID\left(0, \sigma_{S_t}^2\right) \qquad (2.1) $$

where

$$
\begin{aligned}
\alpha_{s_t} &= \alpha_0 \left(1 - S_t\right) + \alpha_1 S_t \\
\beta_{s_t} &= \beta_0 \left(1 - S_t\right) + \beta_1 S_t \\
\sigma_{s_t}^2 &= \sigma_0^2 \left(1 - S_t\right) + \sigma_1^2 S_t
\end{aligned}
\qquad (2.2)
$$

---

[e] Dekker *et al.* [2001] state that generalized impulse response provides more realistic results than orthogonalized impulse response in the context of the linkages among Asian markets.

$S_t = 0$ or 1 is an unobserved state variable representing the stock market regime, α and β are a state-dependent constant term and the autoregressive coefficient, respectively, and σ^2 is a variance of disturbance term ε_t that is normally and independently distributed. In the following empirical analysis, the smoothed state probability for the high volatility regime derived from this model is included in the structural VAR system.

Table 2.1 reports the estimation results of the Markov-switching model comprising Eq. (2.1) and (2.2) for S&P500 index returns. In regime 0 (low volatility regime), all coefficients are statistically significant at the 1% level. However, in regime 1 (high volatility regime), α is not statistically significant, and β is barely statistically significant at the 10% level. α is positive in regime 0 and is negative in regime 1. β is negative in both regime 0 and regime 1. σ^2 in regime 1 is about six times larger than that in regime 0.

Figure 2.1 illustrates time series plots of the smoothed state probability for the high volatility regime together with the S&P500 index. The sharp rises in smoothed state probability coincide closely with the periods of downturn in the S&P500 index, suggesting that state probability adequately captures the turning point of the stock market.

In the next step, we conduct principal component analysis[f] to create the variable designated for tightness of financial condition in the US. Figure 2.2 illustrates the first principal component extracted from a group of risk indicators, namely, TED spread, term spread[g], default premium[h], and volatility index (VIX)[i]. We interpret and use this variable to aggregate overall financial market tightness in the US. As seen in

---

[f] We stationarize and standardize each data series before extracting the first principal component.

[g] Term spread is defined as a yield spread between Treasuries of 10-year constant maturity and 3-month constant maturity.

[h] Default premium is defined as a yield spread between Baa-ranked corporate bond and 10-year Treasury constant maturity.

[i] TED spread, term spread, and default premium are from the Federal Reserve Economic Database of St. Louis FED, and VIX index is from the Chicago Board Options Exchange.

Figure 2.2, this variable adequately captures the spike of tension in financial markets after the bankruptcy of Lehman Brothers Inc.

Table 2.1. Markov-switching estimation for S&P500 index return.

	Sample period: 1/19/1990 – 5/30/2014		
	Parameter	Estimate	S.E.
Regime 0 (low volatility)			
	α_0	0.342 ***	0.049
	β_0	-0.130 ***	0.031
	σ_0^2	2.190 ***	0.107
Regime 1 (high volatility)			
	α_1	-0.237	0.211
	β_1	-0.075 *	0.042
	σ_1^2	12.066 ***	0.609
Transition probability P_{ij}: j to i		$j = 0$	$j = 1$
	$i = 0$	0.980	0.045
	$i = 1$	0.020	0.955
Average duration (Weeks)			
	S_0	51.265	
	S_1	22.289	

Notes: This table reports the estimation results of the Markov-switching model for the S&P500 index return. *, ** and *** denote statistical significance at the 10%, 5% and 1%, respectively.

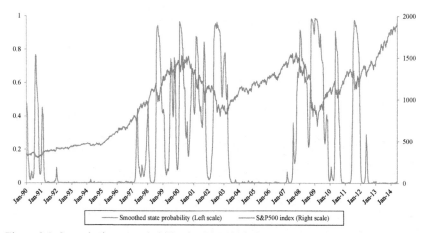

Figure 2.1. Smoothed state probability for S&P500 index return: $S_t = 1$
Notes: The figure displays the smoothed state probability ($S_t = 1$) for S&P500 index return derived from Markov-switching first-order autoregressive (MS(2)-AR(1)) model.

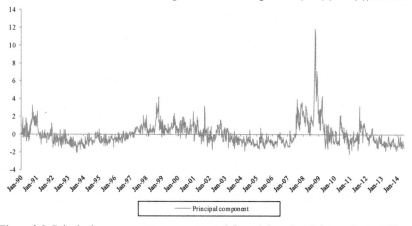

Figure 2.2. Principal component as an aggregated financial market tightness in the US
Notes: The figure illustrates the first principal component extracted from risk indicators in US financial markets, namely, TED spread, term spread, default spread, and VIX.

2.4 Data

In this section, we present data used below. To avoid the bias of estimates accompanying the adjustment of trading hours, we use weekly data rather than daily data. The longest sample is from January 1990 to May 2014[j]. The gold data are the PM fixing prices of the London Bullion Market Association, and we signify gold return with *Gold*. The S&P500 index (*SPX*) is used as the US stock market return. For Asian stock market returns, we use Korea Composite Stock Price Index (*KPI*) for Korea, Jakarta Stock Exchange Composite Index (*JCI*) for Indonesia, Set Index (*SET*) for Thailand, Kuala Lumpur Composite Index (*KLS*) for Malaysia, Philippines Stock Exchange Index (*PSI*) for the Philippines, Hang Seng Index (*HSI*) for Hong Kong, Taiwan Capitalization Weighted Stock Index (*TWI*) for Taiwan, and Straits Times Index (*STI*) for Singapore. We obtain all stock price data from Datastream, and transform it into return series by taking log-difference, $(ln\ X_t - ln\ X_{t-1}) * 100$, where X_t is the PM gold fixing price, or the US or an East Asian stock index. Stock indices for East Asian countries are quoted in US dollars.

Table 2.2 provides the summary statistics for gold and stock return data. The highest mean is seen in Hong Kong, whereas Taiwan experiences the lowest and sole negative mean. Taiwan also records the largest maximum return and standard deviation, showing that the Taiwanese stock market is highly volatile in this sample period. Meanwhile, the largest minimum return appears in Thailand. All return series exhibit negative skewness and excess kurtosis. Reflecting these characteristics, a Jarque-Bera test rejects the null of normality of distribution.

2.5 Empirical Analysis

2.5.1 *Baseline model*

---

[j] Due to data availability, the samples start from April 1990 in Indonesia and from November 1999 in Singapore.

Our baseline structural VAR model is given by:

$$
\begin{bmatrix} PC_t \\ \pi_{1,t} \\ SPX_t \\ Local\,return_t \\ Gold_t \end{bmatrix} = \Phi_0 + \sum_{i=1}^{p} \Phi_i \begin{bmatrix} PC_{t-i} \\ \pi_{1,t-i} \\ SPX_{t-i} \\ Local\,return_{t-i} \\ Gold_{t-i} \end{bmatrix} + \mathbf{v}_t, \qquad (2.3)
$$

Table 2.2. Summary statistics for gold and stock indices

	Gold	SPX	KPI	JCI	SET
Mean	0.088	0.133	0.061	0.163	0.034
Median	0.140	0.241	0.216	0.300	0.305
Maximum	13.197	11.356	17.436	18.803	21.838
Minimum	-8.981	-20.084	-22.929	-23.297	-28.011
Std. Dev.	2.212	2.331	3.890	3.705	3.933
Skewness	-0.032	-0.737	-0.397	-0.380	-0.452
Kurtosis	6.223	9.789	7.350	7.917	9.287
Jarque-Bera	551.334	2560.036	1036.144	1289.202	2139.828
p-value	0.000	0.000	0.000	0.000	0.000
Num. of Obs.	1,273	1,273	1,272	1,250	1,273
	KLS	PSI	HSI	TWI	STI
Mean	0.092	0.139	0.165	-0.007	0.055
Median	0.240	0.231	0.310	0.269	0.160
Maximum	24.579	16.185	13.917	24.762	15.321
Minimum	-19.027	-21.985	-19.921	-24.612	-16.468
Std. Dev.	2.924	3.621	3.419	4.049	2.754
Skewness	-0.010	-0.372	-0.399	-0.253	-0.410
Kurtosis	11.914	7.220	5.908	8.279	8.240
Jarque-Bera	4211.299	973.089	482.303	1472.914	901.284
p-value	0.000	0.000	0.000	0.000	0.000
Num. of Obs.	1,272	1,272	1,273	1,257	769

Notes: This table reports the descriptive statistics for return series used following empirical analysis. The p-value corresponds to the Jarque-Bera test statistic.

where *PC* is the first principal component extracted from a group of risk indicators, namely, TED spread, term spread, default premium, and VIX as explained in the previous section; π_1 is the smoothed state probability of regime 1 (high volatility) for S&P500 index return derived from Eq. (2.1) and (2.2); *SPX* is the S&P500 index return; *Local return* is the individual Asian stock market return; *Gold* is the gold return; Φ_0 and Φ_i are coefficient matrices; and v_t is the matrix of disturbances. As mentioned above, we employ a generalized impulse response that is independent of the order of variables [Koop *et al.*, 1996; Pesaran and Shin, 1998][k]. We choose the model based on the Schwarz Bayesian Information Criterion, and select two lags (i.e., $i = 2$) for all countries.

Figure 2.3 describes the generalized impulse response of stock returns in eight East Asian countries to selected shocks (*PC*, π_1, *SPX* and *Gold*) up to 12 periods ahead. The impulse responses to each shock are very close in shape across countries.

First, although financial market tightening in the US dampens returns in East Asian stock markets, its effect is temporary (i.e., is contained within three weeks). According to the impulse response, the initial impact of *PC* shock is larger in Korea and Singapore than in other markets, implying that these countries are more vulnerable to financial market tightening in the US. Conversely, the impact is relatively small in Malaysia and Taiwan. Second, π_1 shock also depresses East Asian stock returns, with a one-week delay on average. In contrast with the short-lived effects of financial market tightening shock, π_1 shock exerts a significant effect on East Asian stock market returns for a month and a half to two months. The instantaneous magnitude of impulse response to *PC* shock is two to three times larger than to π_1 shock. Third, East Asian stock markets significantly and positively respond to *SPX* shock for about three weeks. The Korean market exhibits large negative responses to *PC* and π_1 shocks, and a positive response to *SPX* shock. This finding suggests that Korea is exposed to higher risk of influence by US financial markets trends. Lastly, a shock to gold return significantly and instantaneously pushes up stock returns in all East Asian countries. The

---

[k] The results presented below, however, are almost same to the results under Choleski decomposition in Eq. (2.3).

largest impulse response is seen in Indonesia. This result is probably due to the fact that Indonesia is a large market for gold.

Now, we turn to the results of forecast error variance decomposition. Table 2.3 provides the results of variance decomposition of respective East Asian stock returns. As with the impulse response analysis, the results are qualitatively similar across countries. The column showing the contribution of the US for each country in Table 2.3 is the summation of relative variance contributions for *PC*, π_1 and *SPX*.

The forecast error variance of returns in East Asian stock markets is predominantly due to own-market variances, and the contribution of other factors is minor except for Korea, Hong Kong, and Singapore. These three markets have high relative variance contribution of financial market tightness and stock return in the US in comparison with other East Asian countries. These results are consistent with the impulse response analysis described above, and are attributable to the fact that Korea, Hong Kong, and Singapore possess advanced financial markets and are therefore more integrated with the US financial market. On the contrary, in Indonesia, Malaysia, and Taiwan, the larger fraction of forecast error variance is accounted for by own-market variance. Thus, it appears that, to some extent, these countries are insulated from the US financial market.

Additionally, we estimate an alternative structural VAR model that replaces *Gold* with the return of West Texas Intermediate (*WTI*). This modification, however, does not bring about major changes in the results obtained above.

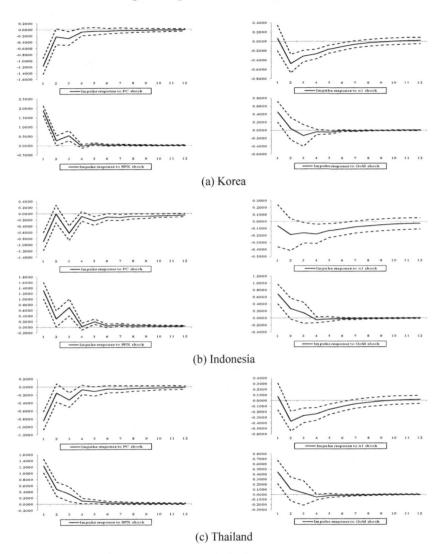

(a) Korea

(b) Indonesia

(c) Thailand

Figure 2.3. Generalized impulse responses of East Asian stock market returns to selected shocks: Baseline model

Notes: The figures illustrate the generalized impulse responses of each East Asian stock market return to one standard deviation shock for selected variables (US aggregated financial market tightness, PC; smoothed state probability for high volatility regime in US stock market, π_1; S&P500 index return, SPX; and gold return, $Gold$, shocks.) Confidence intervals are obtained using the Monte Carlo method with 1,000 replications.

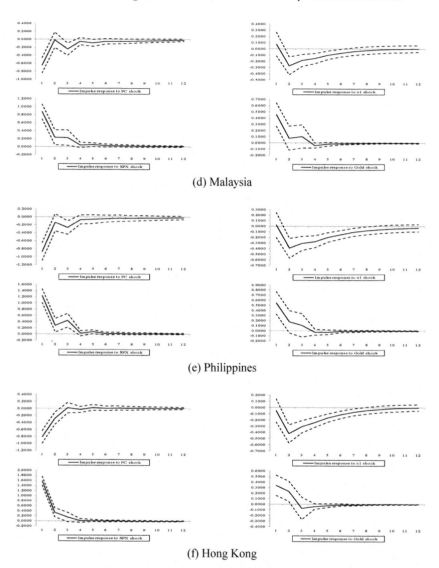

(d) Malaysia

(e) Philippines

(f) Hong Kong

Figure 2.3. (*Continued*)

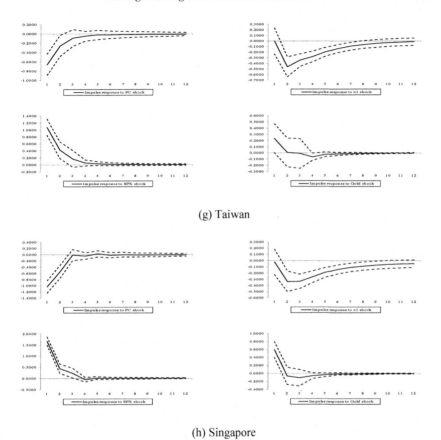

(g) Taiwan

(h) Singapore

Figure 2.3. (*Continued*)

Table 2.3. Forecast error variance decomposition: Baseline model.

Market	Forecast horizon (in weeks)	PC	π_1	SPX	Local return	Gold	Cont. of the US
Korea	1	5.881	0.066	10.385	83.667	0.000	16.333
	3	6.144	1.328	10.805	81.568	0.154	18.278
	6	6.152	1.767	10.795	81.122	0.164	18.714
	12	6.165	1.787	10.791	81.093	0.164	18.743
Indonesia	1	2.848	0.002	3.893	93.258	0.000	6.742
	3	4.005	0.183	4.781	90.602	0.429	8.969
	6	4.231	0.368	4.784	90.185	0.431	9.384
	12	4.371	0.413	4.777	90.008	0.430	9.561
Thailand	1	3.932	0.070	5.454	90.545	0.000	9.455
	3	4.442	1.103	6.444	87.932	0.080	11.989
	6	4.528	1.563	6.427	87.392	0.090	12.518
	12	4.573	1.586	6.422	87.328	0.090	12.582
Malaysia	1	3.478	0.094	3.850	92.578	0.000	7.422
	3	3.876	0.932	4.328	90.731	0.134	9.136
	6	3.963	1.226	4.312	90.357	0.142	9.501
	12	4.020	1.244	4.309	90.285	0.142	9.573
Philippines	1	5.264	0.033	6.354	88.349	0.000	11.651
	3	5.652	1.574	7.193	85.319	0.261	14.420
	6	5.661	2.436	7.139	84.500	0.265	15.235
	12	5.678	2.594	7.125	84.339	0.264	15.397
Hong Kong	1	5.951	0.001	16.606	77.442	0.000	22.558
	3	6.340	2.246	16.400	74.275	0.739	24.986
	6	6.301	3.050	16.264	73.643	0.742	25.615
	12	6.302	3.122	16.250	73.584	0.742	25.675
Taiwan	1	2.527	0.007	4.642	92.824	0.000	7.176
	3	2.848	1.755	5.107	90.278	0.011	9.711
	6	2.844	2.467	5.070	89.593	0.026	10.381
	12	2.845	2.554	5.065	89.510	0.026	10.464

(Continued)

Table 2.3. (*Continued*)

Market	Forecast horizon (in weeks)	PC	π_1	SPX	Local return	Gold	Cont. of the US
				Shock to			
Singapore	1	12.539	0.008	21.487	65.966	0.000	34.034
	3	14.830	2.249	20.840	61.882	0.200	37.919
	6	14.636	3.535	20.638	60.977	0.214	38.809
	12	14.586	3.885	20.562	60.752	0.214	39.033

Notes: This table reports the forecast error variance decomposition of respective East Asian stock market return to each Choleski-factored shock. The order of variables in the structural VAR specification is {PC, π_1, SPX, Local return, Gold}. The column 'Cont. of the US' refers to the summation of relative variance contributions for PC, π_1 and SPX.

2.5.2 East Asia-augmented model

In the following subsection, we estimate the augmented model that incorporates the interaction between regional factors in East Asia and stock returns in each country into the model. The estimated model is represented by:

$$
\begin{bmatrix}
PC_t \\
\pi_{1,t} \\
SPX_t \\
\theta_{1,t/j} \\
Asia\,return_{t/j} \\
Local\,return_t \\
Gold_t
\end{bmatrix}
= \Phi_0 + \sum_{i=1}^{p} \Phi_i
\begin{bmatrix}
PC_t \\
\pi_{1,t} \\
SPX_t \\
\theta_{1,t/j} \\
Asia\,return_{t/j} \\
Local\,return_t \\
Gold_t
\end{bmatrix}
+ v_t,
\tag{2.4}
$$

where $Asia\,return_{t/j}$ is the first principal component extracted from returns in seven East Asian stock markets excluding own market, j, at time t; and $\theta_{1,t/j}$ is the corresponding smoothed state probability for a high volatility regime, obtained in the same way as $\pi_{1,t}$. These procedures enable us to incorporate regional market factors in East Asia without adding too many variables to the VAR system.

Figure 2.4 and Table 2.4 display the results of generalized impulse response and variance decomposition respectively, derived from estimating Eq. (2.4). The shapes of impulse responses in Figure 2.4 (*PC*, π_1, *SPX*, θ_{1j} and *Gold*) are similar to those of the baseline model in Figure 2.3. In this augmented model, however, impulse responses of each return in East Asian stock markets to US financial shocks (e.g., *PC*, π_1 and *SPX*) become somewhat more persistent in several countries in comparison with the baseline model. In particular, impulse responses to π_1 shock do not converge to zero in Malaysia and the Philippines, even 12 periods ahead. Similarly, shock to θ_{1j} is long-lasting in Indonesia. The largest negative response to π_1 and θ_{1j} shocks appears in Korea. These results tell us that Korea is vulnerable not only to US stock market stress, but also to East Asia-regional stock market stress; that is, the Korean stock market is dependent on external market conditions. On the other hand, Indonesia, Malaysia, and the Philippines are immune to regional market stress. To save space, impulse responses to *Asia return$_{lj}$* shock are not displayed in Figure 2.4; however, *Asia return$_{lj}$* shock significantly pushes up stock returns in all East Asian countries for one to two weeks, and its impact is greater than *SPX* shock. Indonesia again shows the largest response to *Gold* shock.

Table 2.4 reports the results of variance decomposition, which are qualitatively similar to those of the baseline model in Table 2.3. The contribution of *Asia return$_{lj}$* is around 20 percent in each country, and it is the largest contributor excluding own shock. The columns showing the contribution of the US and the contribution of East Asia for each country in Table 2.4 are the summations of relative variance contributions for *PC*, π_1 and *SPX*, and for θ_{1j} and *Asia return$_{lj}$*, respectively. We can confirm again that Korea, Hong Kong, and Singapore have comparatively larger contributions from the US, showing qualitatively similar results to those of the baseline model. On the other hand, Indonesia, Malaysia, and the Philippines have comparatively larger contributions from East Asia, which is mainly accounted for by *Asia return$_{lj}$*. Due to differences in sample period, and probably reflecting market integration, the contribution of the US to Taiwan becomes about twice that of the baseline model.

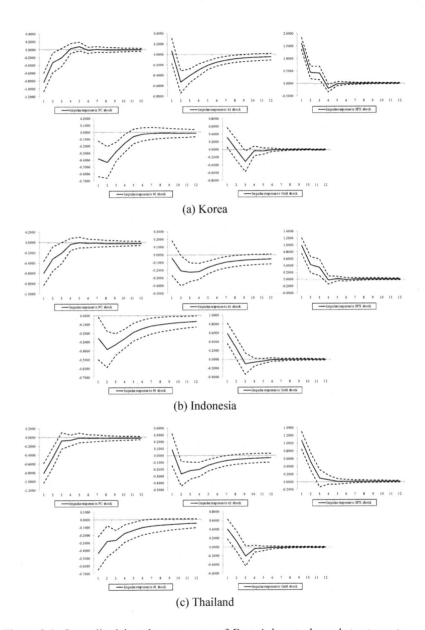

(a) Korea

(b) Indonesia

(c) Thailand

Figure 2.4. Generalized impulse responses of East Asian stock market returns to selected shocks: Asia-augmented model

Notes: The figures illustrate the generalized impulse responses of each East Asian stock market return to one standard deviation shock for selected variables (from left to right, US aggregated financial market tightness, PC; smoothed state probability for high

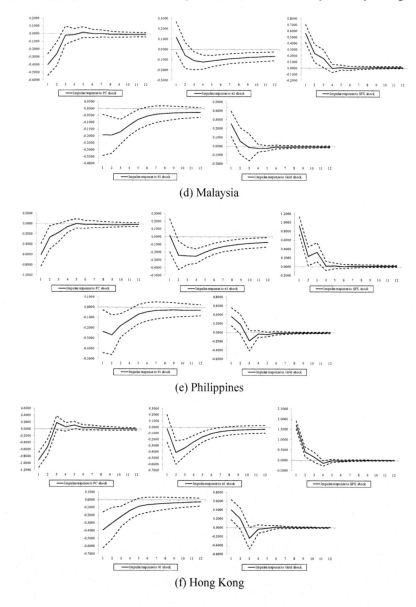

(d) Malaysia

(e) Philippines

(f) Hong Kong

Figure 2.4 (*Continued*). volatility regime in US stock market, p1; S&P500 index return, SPX; smoothed state probability for high volatility regime in East Asia-regional stock market, θ1/j; and gold return, Gold, shocks). Confidence intervals are obtained using the Monte Carlo method with 1,000 replications.

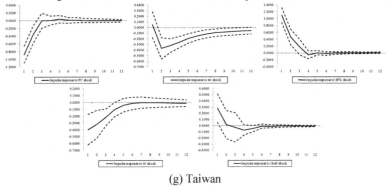

(g) Taiwan

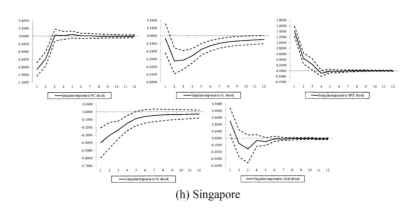

(h) Singapore

Figure 2.4 (*Continued*).

Table 2.4. Forecast error variance decomposition: Asia-augmented model

		Shock to								
Market	Forecast horizon (in weeks)	PC	π_1	SPX	$\theta_{1/j}$	*Asia return$_j$*	*Local return*	*Gold*	Cont. of the US	
Korea	1	5.959	0.115	16.661	0.562	23.118	53.585	0.000	22.735	
	3	6.260	3.213	15.799	1.363	22.039	50.427	0.899	25.272	
	6	6.195	4.310	15.845	1.445	21.704	49.609	0.892	26.350	
	12	6.182	4.554	15.804	1.442	21.649	49.480	0.891	26.539	
Indonesia	1	3.455	0.002	6.196	0.255	22.824	67.269	0.000	9.652	
	3	4.486	0.741	7.245	1.703	21.027	63.788	1.010	12.473	
	6	4.418	1.501	7.148	2.484	20.758	62.677	1.015	13.067	
	12	4.416	1.763	7.102	2.793	20.638	62.280	1.009	13.280	
Thailand	1	6.940	0.179	6.666	1.402	21.009	63.804	0.000	13.785	
	3	8.460	1.181	7.261	2.081	20.059	60.041	0.918	16.902	
	6	8.403	1.831	7.174	2.400	19.908	59.370	0.915	17.407	
	12	8.399	1.965	7.150	2.555	19.849	59.170	0.912	17.514	
Malaysia	1	3.963	0.487	4.594	0.665	17.971	72.320	0.000	9.044	
	3	5.428	0.787	5.375	1.681	17.287	69.293	0.150	11.589	
	6	5.368	1.651	5.319	1.991	17.122	68.387	0.162	12.338	
	12	5.333	2.447	5.274	2.008	16.975	67.801	0.162	13.054	
Philippines	1	4.380	0.027	6.327	0.234	19.617	69.414	0.000	10.734	
	3	5.282	1.255	6.867	0.807	18.549	66.301	0.940	13.404	
	6	5.233	2.623	6.766	0.880	18.362	65.196	0.940	14.622	
	12	5.219	3.203	6.724	0.883	18.251	64.785	0.935	15.146	
Hong Kong	1	8.767	0.007	22.524	0.568	23.007	45.127	0.000	31.298	
	3	10.728	2.524	20.654	1.091	23.050	40.215	1.738	33.906	
	6	10.707	3.396	20.542	1.258	22.779	39.602	1.716	34.645	
	12	10.706	3.538	20.493	1.312	22.728	39.511	1.712	34.737	
Taiwan	1	7.855	0.084	6.453	0.847	22.038	62.724	0.000	14.392	
	3	8.571	2.269	7.175	1.396	21.728	58.761	0.100	18.015	
	6	8.459	3.436	7.130	1.418	21.536	57.893	0.129	19.025	
	12	8.429	3.792	7.103	1.418	21.453	57.676	0.129	19.324	
Singapore	1	11.180	0.000	19.747	0.877	27.293	40.902	0.000	30.927	

Table 2.4. (*Continued*)

Forecast horizon (in weeks)	PC	π_1	SPX	$\theta_{1/j}$	Asia return$_{/j}$	Local return	Gold	Cont. of the US	Cont. of East Asia
				Shock to					
3	14.420	2.494	18.674	1.659	25.791	36.484	0.478	35.588	27.450
6	14.102	3.920	18.374	1.868	25.457	35.787	0.491	36.397	27.325
12	14.040	4.282	18.289	1.912	25.350	35.637	0.490	36.611	27.262

Notes: This table reports the forecast error variance decomposition of respective East Asian stock market returns to each Choleski-factored shock. The order of variables in the structural VAR specification is (PC, π_1, SPX, $\theta_{1/j}$, Asia return/j, Local return, Gold). The columns 'Cont. of the US' and 'Cont. of East Asia' refer to the summation of relative variance contributions for PC, π_1 and SPX, and for $\theta_{1/j}$ and *Asia return*$_{/j}$, respectively.

2.6 Conclusions

In this chapter, we analyze the effects of change in stock market stress and financial market tightness in the US, and shocks in gold return, on East Asian stock markets, based on a structural VAR model. The main results obtained from the empirical analysis above are as follows.

• According to the impulse response derived from our structural VAR model, East Asian stock markets show largely similar responses to each shock. Financial market tightening in the US dampens East Asian stock returns immediately and significantly. In addition, the upsurge of smoothed state probability for a high volatility regime in the US stock market moderately and significantly depresses stock returns for a month and a half to two months, with a short lag. In all East Asian countries, shock to gold return raises stock returns immediately and significantly.

• For the forecast error variance decomposition, East Asian stock markets again show similar results across countries. The forecast error variance for East Asian stock returns are predominantly due to own-market variance, and the contributions of other factors are relatively small. In Korea, Hong Kong, and Singapore, however, the relative variance contributions of financial market tightness and stock return in the US are high in comparison with other East Asian countries. This finding is attributable to the fact that these three economies possess advanced financial markets and therefore are more integrated with the US financial market. Meanwhile, the contribution of gold return to stock market movements is substantially limited in terms of error variance.

Our empirical results confirm that US financial markets still have significant influence on East Asian stock markets, which reinforces findings in the existing literature. In some East Asian countries, however, regional market factors are more important than those emanating from the US.

References

Bessler, D.A. and Yang, J. (2003). The structure of interdependence in international stock markets, *Journal of International Money & Finance*, 22, pp.261–287.

Billio, M. and Pelizzon, L. (2003). Contagion and interdependence in stock markets: Have they been misdiagnosed?, *Journal of Economics and* Business, 55, pp.405–426.

Cha, B. and Oh, S. (2000). The relationship between developed equity markets and the Pacific Basin's emerging equity markets, *International Review of Economics and Finance*, 9, pp.299–322.

Chiang, T.C., Jeon, B.N. and Li, H. (2007). Dynamic correlation analysis of financial contagion: Evidence from Asian markets, *Journal of International Money & Finance*, 26, pp.1206–1228.

Chuang, I-Y., Lu, J-R. and Tswei, K. (2007). Interdependence of international equity variances: Evidence from East Asian markets, *Emerging Markets Review*, 8, pp.311–327.

Corsetti, G., Pericoli, M. and Sbracia, M. (2005). 'Some contagion, some interdependence': More pitfalls in tests of financial contagion, *Journal of International Money & Finance*, 24, pp.1177–1199.

Darrat, A.F. and Zhong, M. (2002). Permanent and transitory driving forces in the Asian - Pacific stock markets, *Financial Review*, 37, pp.35–51.

Dekker, A., Sen, K. and Young, M.R. (2001). Equity market linkages and in the Asia Pacific region: A comparison of the orthogonalised and generalised VAR approach, *Global Finance Journal*, 12, pp.1–33.

Diebold, F.X. and Yilmaz, K. (2009). Measuring financial asset return and volatility spillovers, with application to global equity markets, *The Economic Journal*, 119, pp.158–171.

Domanski, D. and Heath, A. (2007). Financial investors and commodity markets. *BIS Quarterly Review*, 3, pp.53–67.

Engle, R. (2002). Dynamic conditional correlation: A simple class of multivariate generalized autoregressive conditional heteroskedasticity models, *Journal of Business & Economic Statistics*, 20, pp.339–350.

Eun, C.S. and Shim, S. (1989). International transmission of stock market movements, *Journal of Financial and Quantitative Analysis*, 24, pp.241–256.

Forbes, K.J. and Rigobon, R. (2002). No contagion, only interdependence: Measuring stock market comovements, *Journal of Finance*, 57, pp.2223–2261.

Fujiwara, I. and Takahashi, K. (2012). Asian financial linkage: Macro-finance dissonance, *Pacific Economic Review*, 17, pp.136–159.

Gebka, B. and Serwa, D. (2006). Are financial spillovers stable across regimes?, Evidence from the 1997 Asian crisis, *Journal of International Financial Markets, Institutions & Money*, 16, pp.301–317.

Hamao, Y., Masulis, R.W. and Ng, V. (1990). Correlations in price changes and volatility across international stock markets, *Review of Financial studies*, 3, pp.281–307.

Hyde, S., Bredin, D. and Nguyen, N. (2008). Correlation dynamics between Asia-Pacific, EU and US stock returns, *International Finance Review*, 8, pp.39–61.

Koop, G., Pesaran, M.H. and Potter, S.M. (1996). Impulse response analysis in nonlinear multivariate models, *Journal of Econometrics*, 74, pp.119–147.

Liu, Y.A., Pan, M.S. and Shieh, J.C. (1998). International transmission of stock price movements: Evidence from the US and five Asian-Pacific markets, *Journal of Economics and Finance*, 22, pp.59–69.

Masih, A.M.M. and Masih, R. (1997). A comparative analysis of the propagation of stock market fluctuations in alternative models of dynamic causal linkages, *Applied Financial Economics*, 7, pp.59–74.

Masih, R. and Masih, A.M.M. (2001). Long and short term dynamic causal transmission amongst international stock markets, *Journal of International Money & Finance*, 20, pp.563–587.

Miyakoshi, T. (2003). Spillovers of stock return volatility to Asian equity markets from Japan and the US, *Journal of International Financial Markets, Institutions & Money*, 13, pp.383–399.

Miyazaki, T., Toyoshima, Y. and Hamori, S. (2012). Exploring the dynamic interdependence between the gold and other financial markets, *Economics Bulletin*, 32, pp.37–50.

Miyazaki, T. and Hamori, S. (2013). Testing for causality between the gold return and stock market performance: Evidence for 'gold investment in case of emergency', *Applied Financial Economics*, 23, pp.27–40.

Miyazaki, T. and Hamori, S. (2014). Cointegration with regime shift between gold and financial variables, *International Journal of Financial Research*, 5, forthcoming.

Naoui, K., Liouane, N. and Brahim, S. (2010). A dynamic conditional correlation analysis of financial contagion: The case of the subprime credit crisis, *International Journal of Economics and Finance*, 2, pp.85–96.

Park, C.Y., and Mercado Jr, R.V. (2013). Determinants of financial stress in emerging market economies, ADB Economics working paper series No. 356, Asian Development Bank.

Pesaran, H.H. and Shin, Y. (1998). Generalized impulse response analysis in linear multivariate models, *Economics letters*, 58, pp.17–29.

Phylaktis, K., 1999. Capital markets integration in the Pacific Basin region: An impulse response analysis, *Journal of International Money & Finance*, 18, pp.267–287.

Phylaktis, K. and Ravazzolo, F. (2005). Stock market linkages in emerging markets: Implications for international portfolio diversification, *Journal of International Financial Markets, Institutions & Money*, 15, pp.91–106.

Sander, H. and Kleimeier, S. (2003). Contagion and causality: an empirical investigation of four Asian crisis episodes, *Journal of International Financial Markets, Institutions & Money*, 13, pp.171–186.

Sheng, H-C. and Tu, A.H. (2000). A study of cointegration and variance decomposition among national equity indices before and during the period of the Asian financial crisis, *Journal of Multinational Financial Management*, 10, pp.345–365.

Tang, K. and Xiong, W. (2012). Index investment and financialization of commodities, *Financial Analysts Journal*, 68, pp.54–74.

Tytell, I., Elekdag, S., Danninger, S., and Balakrishnan, R. (2009). *The transmission of financial stress from advanced to emerging economies*, International Monetary Fund.

Yang, J., Kolari, J.W. and Min, I. (2003). Stock market integration and financial crises: The case of Asia, *Applied Financial Economics*, 13, pp.477–486.

Yang, J., Hsiao, C., Li, Q. and Wang, Z. (2006). The emerging market crisis and stock market linkages: Further evidence, *Journal of Applied Econometrics*, 21, pp.727–744.

Yiu, M.S., Ho, W.Y.A. and Choi, D.F. (2010). Dynamic correlation analysis of financial contagion in Asian markets in global financial turmoil, *Applied Financial Economics*, 20, pp.345–354.

Chapter 3

Business Cycle Volatility and Hot Money in Emerging East Asian Markets

Xiaojing Cai

Graduate School of Economics, Kobe University

2-1, Rokkodai, Nada-Ku, Kobe 657-8501, Japan

Email: saisizuka@gmail.com

Shigeyuki Hamori

Faculty of Economics, Kobe University

2-1, Rokkodai, Nada-Ku, Kobe 657-8501, Japan

Email: hamori@econ.kobe-u.ac.jp

3.1 Introduction

Over the previous decades, East Asia has emerged as the world's fastest-growing regional economy and become one of the three core economic regions (along with Europe and North America) [Dent 2013]. The cooperation and integration through trade, foreign investment, and international finance in East Asia have increasingly matured. The region's miraculous economic growth and dynamism has become a popular topic for academic and business research. Furthermore, its growing global significance lies not just in developed economies like Japan, but also in emerging economies like Thailand, Malaysia, South Korea, and Indonesia.

As mentioned above, most countries in East Asia are still characterized as emerging countries or small open economies susceptible to huge capital inflows and outflows. Such international capital flows that cannot be explained by trade surpluses, foreign direct investments, or growth of foreign exchange reserves are referred to as "hot money" [Guo and Huang 2010]. Since hot money instantaneously moves in and out of countries with higher interest rates and/or expected changes in exchange rates, international investors can achieve substantial gains by transferring money between different countries with different interest rates.

However, significant hot money flows may affect a country's balance of payments and potentially lead to market instability. Stiglitz [1999] indicated that short-term capital flows ("hot money") could increase the fragility of the financial system and destabilize the economy. In particular, during 1997–1998, much of the emerging East Asian region was engulfed in an unprecedented financial crisis. According to Chari and Kehoe [2003], economic booms and crises in emerging economies are closely linked to international capital flows. That is, while large capital flows into a small open market may lead to economic booms; this phenomenon may give rise to economic contractions as well.

In the economic literature, several researchers believe that hot money can provide a plausible explanation for business cycle volatility. Ferreira and Matos [2008] suggested that international institutional investors are more prone to chase shares with recent positive stock return performance in emerging markets, and this phenomenon may be referred to as herding behavior. The East Asia currency crisis of 1997 may be cited as an example of this phenomenon. Calvo [1998] suggested that since the outflow of hot money tends to occur swiftly and simultaneously, a country's economic crisis might be driven by herding behavior that is not necessarily linked to macroeconomic fundamentals. Therefore, it should be noted that speculative capital flows might have a more significant impact on business cycle volatility for emerging markets such as Thailand, Malaysia, South Korea, and Indonesia.

Several studies in the literature have focused on the determinants of the level or volatility of short-term capital flows or their effects on the host country and its financial stability [Ferreira and Laux 2009; Edison and Reinhart 2001]. However, it is also important to examine the linkage between hot money and business cycle volatility in recipient countries. Guo and Huang [2010] use a structural vector error correction model to investigate this linkage in China and find clear evidence of a considerable degree of long-run cointegration and bidirectional causality effects between hot money and business cycle volatility.

In contrast to the vector autoregressive (VAR) model used by Guo and Huang [2010], we consider speculative capital flow effects across different business cycles based on state-dependent models. We employ the Markov-switching intercept autoregressive heteroskedasticity VAR (MSIAH-VAR) model [Guidolin and Timmermann 2006; Ang and Timmermann 2012] to examine the effect of hot money on emerging markets. Yang and Hamori [2014] investigate the spillover effect from the US monetary policy to selected ASEAN stock markets by employing MSIAH-VAR models and confirm the existence of two distinct regimes for both the US monetary policy and the stock markets. Simo-Kengne *et al.* [2013] use the Markov-switching vector autoregressive (MS-VAR) model to examine asymmetries in the impact of monetary policy on the middle segment of the South African housing market from 1966 to 2011 and suggest that the impact of monetary policy is larger in bear regime than in bull regime.

The purpose of this study is to develop a framework to analyze the importance of hot money in driving the GDP growth of East Asian emerging markets. Since hot money flows in emerging countries are largely affected by the US short-term interest rate, we also investigate the effect of the US short-term interest rate on hot money flows. In addition, we examine whether this impact differs across economic regimes of low and high volatility growth.

The remainder of this paper is organized as follows. In Section 3.2, a regime-switching three-dimensional VAR model is estimated for

Thailand, Malaysia, South Korea, and Indonesia. Section 3.3 describes our data sets and descriptive statistics. Section 3.4 presents our empirical results. Finally, Section 3.5 concludes.

3.2 Model Specification

3.2.1 *The MSIAH-VAR model*

The MSIAH-VAR model can be defined by equations as follows:

$$y_t = \mu_{s_t} + \sum_{k=1}^{p} \varnothing_{k,s_t} y_{t-k} + u_t, \quad u_t \sim i.i.d.N(0, \Sigma_{s_t}) \tag{3.1}$$

where y_t refers to a vector that depends on the regime $s_t = m$, with $m = 1,2$ and includes three variables the US short-term interest rate, the GDP growth rate, and hot money. μ_{s_t} is a vector of regime intercept terms. $\varnothing_{st}$ is a 3×3 matrix of the autoregressive parameters. Σ_{s_t} is a 3×3 variance-covariance matrix.

Hamilton [1988] proposes the application of unobservable Markovian chains as regime-generating processes.

$$p_{ij} = prob(s_t = j \mid s_{t-1} = i, s_{t-2} = k, \dots) = prob(s_t = j \mid s_{t-1} = i) \tag{3.2}$$

This study assumes the existence of two regimes. Thus, collecting the transition probabilities in a 2×2 matrix gives the transition matrix **P** as follows.

$$\mathbf{P} = \begin{pmatrix} p_{11} & p_{21} = 1 - p_{22} \\ p_{12} = 1 - p_{11} & p_{22} \end{pmatrix} \tag{3.3}$$

where the element of the ith row and jth column describes the transition probability p_{ij}.

A likelihood function of the conditional distribution $f(y_t)$ is derived and maximized in order to obtain parameter estimates of the MSIAH-VAR model. The likelihood function $L(\theta \mid y_t)$ is given by

$$L(\theta \mid y_t) = \sum_{t=1}^{T} \ln f(y_t \mid y_{t-1}) \tag{3.4}$$

with

$$f(y_t \mid y_{t-1};\theta) = \sum_{m=1}^{2} f(y_t \mid y_{t-1}, s_t = m;\theta) prob(s_t = m \mid y_{t-1};\theta) \qquad (3.5)$$

The nonlinear expectation-maximization (EM) algorithm proposed by Krolzig [1997] is applied to estimate the parameters.

$$\hat{\theta}_{ML} = argmaxL(\theta \mid y_t) \qquad (3.6)$$

where the vector θ includes the MSIAH-VAR parameters (μ_{St}, $\varnothing_{St}, \Sigma_{St.}$ and the transition probability matrix **P**) to be estimated.

3.2.2 Regime-dependent impulse response functions

We employ impulse response functions to track down the magnitude and the persistence of each variable's response to economic shocks—hot money shock, GDP growth rate shock, and the US short-term interest rate shock—over time. This method was developed by Ehrmann *et al.* [2001].

The element y_t can be written in the following form as

$$y_t = \mu_{s_t} + u_t + \varphi_1 u_{t-1} + \varphi_2 u_{t-2} + \cdots \qquad (3.7)$$

with

$$\varphi_k = \frac{\partial y_{t+k}}{\partial u_t}\bigg|_{s_t} = \cdots = s_{t+k} = m \quad for \ k \geq 0 \qquad (3.8)$$

where the element of φ_k as a function of the response's time horizon k is the impulse response function and describes the response of $y_{i,t+k}$ to a one-time impulse of one standard deviation in $u_{j,t}$ in regime m.

According to Ehrmann *et al.* [2001], the regime-dependent impulse response function φ_k can be estimated through the standard bootstrapping technique. In addition, we obtain the confidence bands by Markov chain Monte Carlo (MCMC) simulation with Gibbs sampling of 5,000 draws with a burn-in of 2000.

3.3 Data

This paper uses quarterly data from the first quarter of 1981 to that of 2014 for the four emerging East Asian countries to analyze the linkage among the US short-term interest rate, GDP growth rate and hot money using the MSIAH-VAR model. We use the first difference estimate of the US short-term interest rate (ΔUSST rate) to eliminate the unit root effect and apply the GDP growth rate for the four East Asian countries to represent the business cycle.

$$\text{GDP growth rate}(\Delta\,GDP\%) = GDP_t\,/\,GDP_{t-1} - 1 \qquad (3.9)$$

The instantaneous mobility of hot money flows between financial markets and its poor monitoring make it difficult to find a well-defined method to estimate such flows. In this study, we follow Martin and Morrison [2008] to calculate the hot money flows.

Hot money flows (HM in US$bn) = changes in foreign exchange rate − balance of trade − foreign direct investment.

All data sets are obtained from Datastream. Table 3.1 shows the summary statistics of raw data and the results of unit root test. From Table 3.1, we can see that the GDP growth rates of the four emerging East Asian countries are similar (approximately at the level of 2%). Hot money flows for all the four markets are negative. The figures for Thailand and South Korea are both about −0.6 US$bn and those for Malaysia and Indonesia reach about −4.0 US$bn. The Jarque-Bera (J-B) test statistics imply a rejection at the 1% level of the null hypothesis that the two variables and the US short-term interest rate are normally distributed for all the four countries. We also use Phillips–Perron (PP) [Phillips and Perron 1988] test to conduct the unit root test of HM, ΔGDP, and ΔUSST. From Table 3.1, it is clear that all variables are stationary at the 1% level.

Figure 3.1 presents the quarterly data series of the US short-term interest rate, GDP growth rate, and hot money for the four selected emerging East Asian countries. Figure 3.1 clearly shows that the volatility of GDP growth rate synchronizes with that of hot money, while the changes in the US short-term interest rate are inversely proportional to those in the hot money flows.

Table 3.1. Descriptive statistics and unit root test results.

		Obs.	Mean	Std.Dev.	Skewness	Kurtosis	J-B	PP test
Thailand	ΔGDP (%)	132	1.965	5.171	−1.074	4.140	119.6***	−8.94***
	HM (bn)	132	−0.625	3.298	−0.233	6.865	260.4***	−10.94***
Malaysia	ΔGDP (%)	132	2.036	5.293	−1.157	2.774	71.81***	−8.658***
	HM (bn)	132	−4.115	4.908	−1.790	7.154	352.1***	−7.204***
Korea	ΔGDP (%)	132	2.425	5.248	−3.341	17.998	2027***	−8.00***
	HM (bn)	132	−0.600	6.397	−2.715	16.644	1685***	−7.404***
Indonesia	ΔGDP (%)	132	2.148	9.406	−0.327	11.510	731.1***	−10.228***
	HM (bn)	132	−3.470	2.981	−1.632	4.048	148.7***	−6.414***
US	ΔUSST rate	132	−0.127	0.71	−2.097	7.994	448.2***	−8.77***

Notes: ΔGDP indicates GDP growth rate, HM denotes hot money, and ΔUSST rate denotes the first difference of the US short-term interest rate. bn in parentheses represents billion US dollars. Obs. is the sample size and Std.Dev. stands for standard deviation; *** denotes the significance at the 1% level; J-B corresponds to Jarque–Bera test statistics that are all significant at the 1% level; PP test presents the results of Phillips-Perron test, which implies the null hypothesis that unit root is present is rejected at the 1% level in all cases.

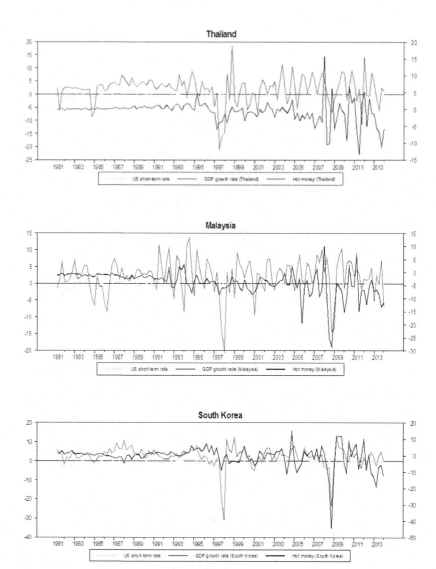

Figure 3.1. Quality data series from 1981:Q1 to 2014:Q1

Notes: Including the first difference of the US short-term interest rate (left scale), GDP growth rates (left scale in percentage)and hot money (right scale in billion US dollars) of the four emerging East Asian countries. All data sets are obtained from Datastream.

Figure 3.1. (*Continued*)

3.4 Empirical Results

3.4.1 *Estimations of the regime-switching model*

In this paper, we first employ the MSIAH-VAR model to estimate the parameters and find the linkage among the GDP growth rate and hot money flows for the selected four emerging East Asian countries and the first difference of the US short-term interest rate (ΔUSST). We focus on two regimes—the tranquil period and the turmoil period. Since the selected markets have all experienced high growth rates in recent years, a specification of the two regimes is applicable to present the real economic situation.

Table 3.2 presents the estimation results for the MSIAH (3)-VAR (1) models for Thailand and Malaysia and Table 3.3 shows those for South Korea and Indonesia. From Table 3.2 and 3.3, we find that the mean of the GDP growth rate is higher with lower volatility in the case of regime 1 than that of regime 2 for the four emerging countries, implying that regime 1 represents the stable period with high and stable economic growth rate. However, both mean and volatility of ΔUSST and hot money are lower in regime 1 as compared to regime 2, which indicate that both ΔUSST and capital flows exercise little influence on a market during the tranquil period.

Table 3.2. MSIAH (3)-VAR (1) models for Thailand and Malaysia.

	Thailand			Malaysia		
	ΔUSST rate	ΔGDP (%)	HM (bn)	ΔUSST rate	ΔGDP (%)	HM (bn)
Regime-dependent intercepts						
μ_1	−0.179** (0.091)	4.779** (2.427)	0.198 (1.041)	−14.735** * (4.94)	8.244*** (1.319)	0.107 (1.13)
μ_2	−0.097 (0.091)	2.264*** (0.548)	0.212 (0.127)	−1.879 (1.525)	1.239* (0.722)	3.267*** (0.571)
Autoregressive parameters						
$\phi_{1,\Delta US\ rate}$	0.465*** (0.065)	0.443 (0.550)	0.008 (0.146)	0.489*** (0.067)	−0.026 (0.020)	0.009 (0.017)
$\phi_{1,\Delta GDP}$	0.003 (0.006)	0.276*** (0.096)	0.028 (0.025)	−0.103 (0.161)	0.228*** (0.078)	−0.058 (0.035)
$\phi_{1,\Delta HM}$	−0.016* (0.009)	0.671*** (0.182)	0.277*** (0.080)	0.263 (0.231)	0.466*** (0.079)	0.729*** (0.059)
Regime 1: Variance						
σ_1	0.325*** (0.052)	8.493*** (1.711)	0.446*** (0.097)	49.777*** (8.136)	17.305** * (3.925)	2.194*** (0.422)
Regime 2: Variance						
σ_2	0.524*** (0.023)	47.508** * (9.335)	28.682** * (6.248)	581.998** * (135.208)	23.102** * (3.995)	66.163*** (13.529)
	Probability		Duration	Probability		Duration
Regime 1	0.886		8.772	0.830		5.882
Regime 2	0.888		8.929	0.916		11.905
LL		−679.288			−1150.299	

Notes: ΔGDP (%) is GDP growth rate in percentage, HM (bn) denotes Hot money in billion US dollars, and ΔUSST rate denotes the first difference of the US short-term interest rate; Duration can be calculated as $\dfrac{1}{1-p_{11(22)}}$; LL represents the log likelihood value. The numbers in parentheses represent standard errors; *, **, and *** denote significance at the 10%, 5%, and 1% levels, respectively.

Tables 3.2 and 3.3 also show the value of transition probabilities and durations based on the MSIAH-VAR model. The duration for regime 1 and that for regime 2 is similar in the case of Thailand. However, the duration for regime 1 is shorter than that for regime 2 in the case of Malaysia, while in cases of South Korea and Indonesia, regime 1 is longer. The economic implication of these statistics for the states is obvious. The duration of the stable period and that of the crisis period is similar in Thailand; however, in Malaysia, the economy has overall experienced more turmoil than stable periods, while the stable period is longer in case of South Korea and Indonesia during our period of observation.

We also plot the smoothed transition probabilities in order to understand the regime properties completely. Figure 3.2 displays the transition probability of regime 1 for the selected emerging countries. From Figure 3.2, we can observe that economies of Thailand and Malaysia experienced high and stable growth before the 1992 oil shock, while those of South Korea and Indonesia were influenced little by this oil shock and maintained a high growth rate before the 1997–1999 Asian currency crisis until the 2008 global financial crisis, when the two regimes occurred alternately. The four emerging countries experienced a period of recession after the global financial crisis of 2008. Especially, Figure 3.2 shows that the two regimes alternated inconspicuously in the four emerging markets during the period of 1985–1986 economic crisis, implying that hot money play an insignificant role in the 1985–1986 economic crisis.

Table 3.3. MSIAH (3)-VAR (1) models for South Korea and Indonesia.

	South Korea			Indonesia		
	ΔUSST rate	ΔGDP (%)	HM (bn)	ΔUSST rate	GDP (%)	HM (bn)
Regime-dependent intercepts						
μ_1	−0.056 (0.068)	2.847*** (0.411)	−0.628 (0.689)	0.022 (0.073)	2.928*** (0.541)	−3.230** * (0.382)
μ_2	0.198 (0.503)	−36.159*** (6.933)	22.077*** (8.065)	−0.583*** (0.169)	−1.992 (3.616)	4.366*** (0.936)
Autoregressive parameters						
$\phi_{1,\Delta US\ rate}$	0.422*** (0.068)	1.001** (0.446)	0.144 (0.706)	0.536*** (0.077)	−1.504 (1.138)	0.089 (0.356)
$\phi_{1,\Delta GDP}$	0.015 (0.010)	0.357*** (0.059)	0.087 (0.106)	0.001 (0.003)	0.030 (0.064)	−0.038** (0.018)
$\phi_{1,\Delta HM}$	−0.008 (0.008)	0.081* (0.044)	0.370*** (0.081)	0.009 (0.012)	0.039 (0.039)	0.563*** (0.059)
Regime 1: Variance						
σ_1	0.221***	6.794***	22.967***	0.111***	24.641**	3.320***

	(0.023)	(0.897)	(2.809)	(0.020)	* (4.063)	(0.492)
Regime 2: Variance						
σ_2	1.026*** (0.981)	387.066 (345.899)	261.487 (214.685)	0.579*** (0.178)	379.525*** (119.690)	21.900*** (3.791)
	Probability	Duration		Probability		Duration
Regime 1	0.927	13.699		0.938		16.129
Regime 2	0.886	8.772		0.906		10.638
LL	−764.109			−756.878		

Notes: ΔGDP (%) is GDP growth rate in percentage, HM (bn) denotes Hot money in billion US dollars, and ΔUSST rate denotes the first difference of the US short-term interest rate; Duration can be calculated as $\dfrac{1}{1-P_{11(22)}}$; LL represents the log likelihood value. The numbers in parentheses represent standard errors; *, **, and *** denote significance at the 10%, 5%, and 1% levels, respectively.

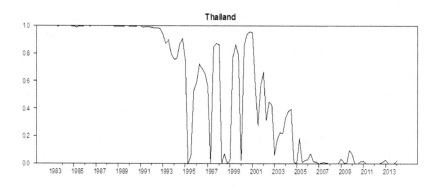

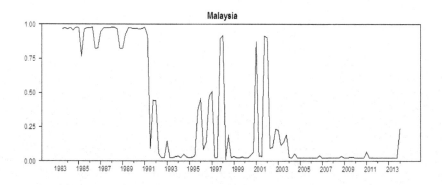

Figure 3.2. MCMC Probability of Regime 1.

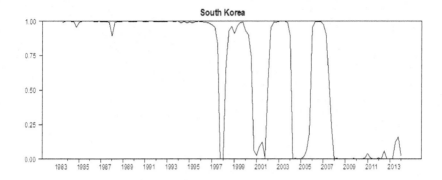

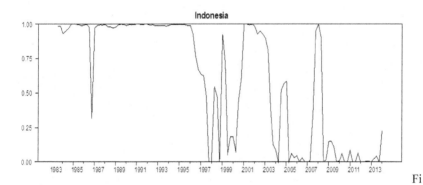

Fi

Figure 3.2. (*Continued*)

3.4.2 *Regime-dependent impulse response functions*

As Tables 3.2 and 3.3 shows the autoregressive coefficients are not statistically significant in any of the cases. Thus, it is difficult to obtain a reliable economic inference relating to the hot money effect. Therefore, in the second step, impulse response functions are computed based on the estimation of the MSIAH-VAR models presented in Figures 3.3, 3.4, and 3.5 in order to gain a comprehensive understanding of how hot money or ΔUSST affect the GDP growth rate or vice versa.

Figure 3.3 presents the impulse response functions of GDP growth rate to a hot money shock. We focus on the magnitude and persistence of the hot money effect on GDP growth in the two different regimes. The figure clearly indicates that when the four emerging countries suffer from a hot money shock, GDP growth rate increased both in regime 1 and regime 2 for Thailand, Malaysia, and Indonesia. In the case of South Korea, however, the shock affects the economic growth rate negatively in regime 1, implying that hot money may not be considered as capital to stimulate GDP growth. Moreover, during the crisis period in regime 2, all the countries suffer from a low GDP growth rate with international capital outflow.

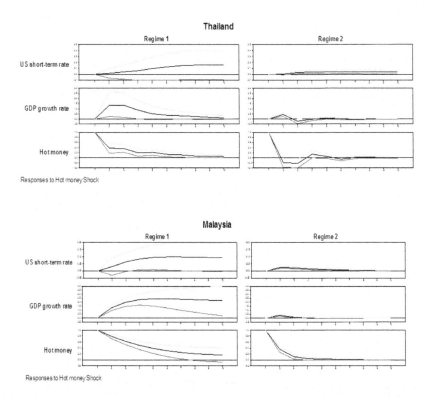

Figure 3.3. Impulse responses of the US short-term interest rate, GDP growth rate, and hot money to a positive hot money shock at regime 1 and regime 2.

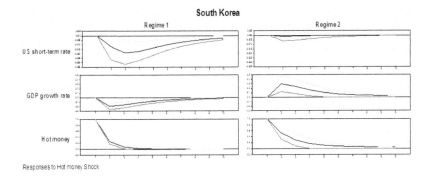

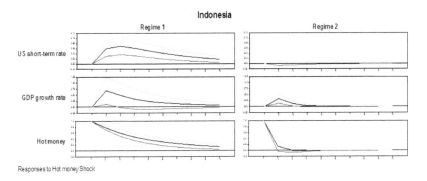

Figure 3.3. (*Continued*)

Figure 3.4 displays the responses of hot money to the GDP growth rate based on the impulse response functions for all the four emerging countries. We also analyze the magnitude and persistence of the GDP growth rate effect in different regimes. In the case of Thailand, a GDP growth rate shock has an insignificant effect on hot money flows in regime 1, while significant positive effects occur in regime 2, after which both effects decrease over time. These results indicate that the Thailand government employs policies to control capital flows during the crisis period. In the cases of Malaysia and South Korea as well, the GDP growth rate has an insignificant effect on hot money flows in regime 1 and then the effect turns negative in regime 2, implying that when the economy of an emerging country enters into recession, international capital flows out from the market correspondingly. In the case of

Indonesia, we find that although the initial effect on hot money is negative, this turns positive over time in regime 1. Then, the Indonesian government employs a capital control policy to stunt capital out from the country in regime 2. Overall, as observed above, hot money flows in the four East Asian emerging countries shows variable behavior during the tranquil and turmoil periods. Thailand and Indonesia both employ policies to control the capital outflow during the turmoil period, while Malaysia and South Korea do not employ any such measures.

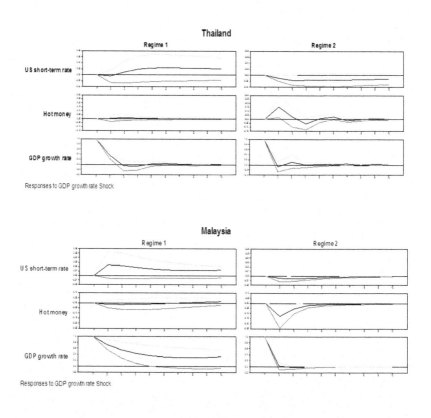

Figure 3.4. Impulse responses of the US short-term interest rate, hot money, and GDP growth rate to a positive GDP growth rate shock at regime 1 and regime 2.

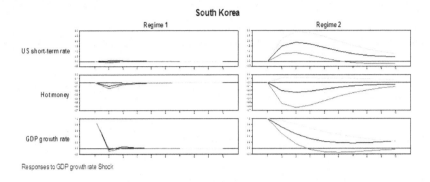

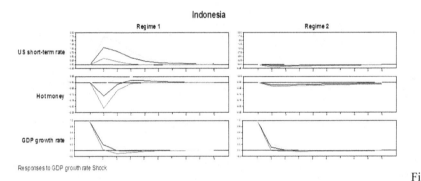

Fi

Figure 3.4. (*Continued*)

In addition, since hot money is sensitive to the US short-term interest rate, we also compute the impulse response functions based on the estimation of the MSIAH-VAR model to analyze the effect of the latter on the former, as shown in Figure 3.5. Figure 3.5 clearly indicates that during the tranquil period in regime 1, an initial US short-term interest rate shock affects hot money inflow positively. In other words, hot money flows in all the selected emerging countries and boosts the economy. Moreover, in the cases of Thailand and Malaysia, hot money inflows decrease during the turmoil period in regime 2 as the US short-term interest rate increases gradually. These results are consistent with the basic economic principle that when the US government maintains a low interest rate level, a large amount of international speculative capital flows in the emerging markets, as investors expect to earn a short-term profit, thereby causing an economic boom in these markets, Later, as the US government increases the interest rate to restrain the boom, international capital flows out of the emerging markets, triggering a crisis in these markets. However, in the case of South Korea and Indonesia, the capital inflows continuously rise in regime 2, indicating that the two countries governments adopt necessary measures to arrest the capital outflow.

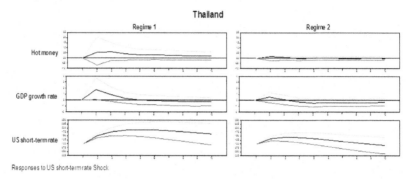

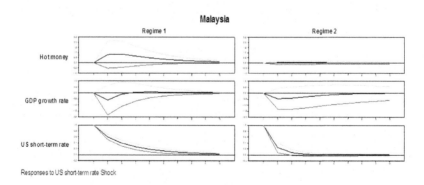

Figure 3.5. Impulse responses of hot money, GDP growth rate and the US short-term interest rate to a positive US short-term interest rate shock at regime 1 and regime 2.

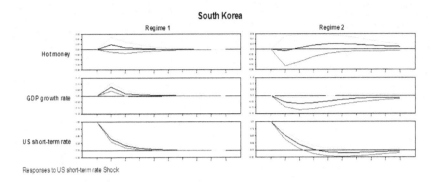

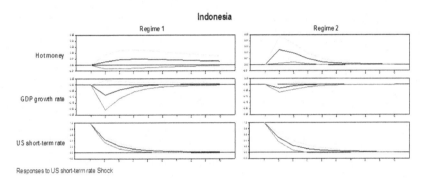

Figure 3.5. (*Continued*)

3.5 Conclusions

In the present study, we employed a two-regime-dependent MSIAH-VAR model to investigate the importance of hot money in driving GDP growth for four emerging East Asian markets–Thailand, Malaysia, South Korea, and Indonesia–during the period 1981–2014. Since hot money flow is sensitive to the US short-term interest rate, we also added the latter as a variable to analyze the linkage among the US short-term interest rate, GDP growth rate and hot money.

We find that the Markov-switching systems are characterized with two distinct regimes—the tranquil period in regime 1 and the turmoil period in regime 2. The results of this study provide a convincing explanation for the state of high volatility that dominated the evolution mainly reflected in the 1992 oil shock, 1997–1999 Asian currency crisis, and the 2008 global financial crisis. In addition, we compute impulse response functions based on the estimation of the MSIAH–VAR models in order to gain a comprehensive understanding of the effect of hot money, the US short-term interest rate, and the GDP growth rate. We find that during the stable period, speculative capital produces an economic boom in Thailand, Malaysia, and Indonesia, while it causes the instability of the economy in South Korea. On the other hand, all the four countries suffer from a low economic growth during the turmoil period. Additionally, with regard to the response pattern of hot money to GDP growth rate, the results obtained for Malaysia and South Korea during the crisis period are consistent with the basic economic principle that when the economy of an emerging country enters into recession, international capital flows out from the market correspondingly. On the other hand, Thailand and Indonesia, employed capital control measures to restrain the capital outflow. Moreover, we analyze the response pattern of hot money to the US short-term interest rate shock for each country and find that hot money inflows increase in all the four emerging countries during the tranquil period and boost the economy. However, hot money inflows decrease during the turmoil period as the US short-term interest rate gradually increases. These results are also in line with the above-mentioned economic principle. The exceptions are South Korea and Indonesia, whose governments adopt certain measures during the turmoil period.

The findings of this study have important implications for policymakers in the East Asian emerging countries. First, since this study proves that intense linkage exists between hot money flows and business cycle in the East Asian emerging countries, the findings could aid the government to analyze the implications of the effect of hot money on economic growth and to adopt necessary measures to reduce the risk of financial instability during the crisis period. In addition, since the effect of the US short-term interest rate on hot money flows is confirmed, indeed, it is critical for policymakers to pay attention to the changes in the US short-term interest rate. In particular, the Thailand and Malaysian governments should employ appropriate policies to reduce hot money outflows during the turmoil period and to stabilize the economy.

References

Ang, A. and Timmerman, A. (2012). Regime changes and financial markets, *Annual Review Financial Economics*, 4, pp.313-337.

Calvo, G. (1998). Capital flows and capital-market crisis: The simple economics of sudden stops, *Journal of Applied Economics*, 1, pp.35-54.

Chari, V.V. and Kehoe, P. (2003). Hot money, *Journal of Political Economy*, 111, pp.1262-1292.

Dent, C.M. (2013). Paths ahead for East Asia and Asia-Pacific regionalism, *International Affairs*, 89, pp.963-985.

Edison, H and Reinhart. C. (2001). Stopping hot money, *Journal of Development Economics*, 66, pp.533-553.

Ehrmann, M., M.Ellison and Valla, N. (2001). Regime-Dependent impulse response function in a Markov-switching vector autoregression model, Discussion Paper No. 11/2001, Bank of Finland.

Ferreira, M. and Laux, P.A. (2009). Portfolio flows, volatility and growth, *Journal of International Money and Finance*, 28, pp.271-292.

Ferreira, M. and Matos, P. (2008). The colors of investors' money: The role of institutional investors around the world, *Journal of Financial Economics*, 88, pp.499-533.

Guidolin, M. and Timmermann, A. (2006). An econometric model of nonlinear dynamics in the joint distribution of stock and bond returns, *Journal of Applied Economics*, 21, pp.1-22.

Guo, F. and Huang, Y. (2010). Hot money and business cycle volatility: Evidence from China, *China and the World Economy*, 18, pp.73-89.

Hamilton, J. D. (1988). Rational expectations econometric analysis of changes in regime: An investigation of the term structure of interest rates, *Journal of Economic Dynamics and Control,* 12, pp.385-423.

Martin, M. and Morrison, W. (2008). China's "hot money" problem, Congressional research service report no. RS22921, Congressional Research Service, Washington, DC.

Krolzig, H-M. (1997). Markov-switching vector autoregressions: modeling, statistical inference and application to business cycle analysis. Lecture Notes in Economics and Mathematical Systems, Springer.

Phillips, P. and Perron, P. (1988). Testing for a unit root in time series regression, *Biometrika*, 75, pp.335-346.

Simo-Kengne, B.D., M. Balcilar, R. Gupta, M. Reid. and Aye, G.C. (2013). Is the relationship between monetary policy and house prices asymmetric across bull and bear markets in South Africa? Evidence from a Markov-switching vector autoregressive model, *Economic Modelling*, 32, pp.161-171.

Stiglitz, J. (1999). Lessons from East Asia, *Journal of Policy Modeling*, 21, pp. 311–330.

Yang, L. and Hamori, S. (2014). Spillover effect of US monetary policy to ASEAN stock markets: Evidence from Indonesia, Singapore, and Thailand, *Pacific-Basin Finance Journal*, 26, pp.145-155.

Part II

Long-Run Economic Consequences of Remittance Inflows and Natural Resource Dependence

Chapter 4

Dynamic Impacts of Remittances on Economic Growth in Asia: Evidence from the Dynamic Heterogeneous Panel

Nannan Yuan

School of Finance, Zhongnan University of Economics and Law

182# Nanhu Avenue, East Lake High-tech Development Zone,

Wuhan 430-073, P.R. China

Email: wsyuanan@znufe.edu.cn

Takeshi Inoue

Faculty of Policy Studies, Nanzan University

Seirei-Cho, Seto 489-0863, Japan

Email: tinoue@ps.nanzan-u.ac.jp

Shigeyuki Hamori

Faculty of Economics, Kobe University

2-1, Rokkodai, Nada-Ku, Kobe 657-8501, Japan

Email: hamori@econ.kobe-u.ac.jp

4.1 Introduction

From 1988 to 2007, remittance inflows to developing countries considerably increased from US$20 billion to US$338 billion. Although remittances fell to US$317 billion in 2009 due to the subprime mortgage crisis in the United States [Ratha *et al.*, 2009], they were estimated to have increased by 6.0%, 6.2%, and 8.1% in 2010, 2011, and 2012, respectively [Wakayama, 2011]. Remittances have become one of the largest and most important inflow resources for developing countries alongside foreign direct investment (FDI) and official development assistance (ODA) [Barajas *et al.*, 2009; Driffield and Jones, 2013]. Figure 4.1 compares the growth rates of ODA, FDI, and remittances in 16 Asian countries from 1986 to 2011. In most years, remittances increased and remained positive overall, which indicates stability. The average growth rate of remittances is approximately 11.59%, which has the similar overall trends with FDI, the average growth rate of 19.98%.

In the global context, Asian countries have become major recipients of remittances because of their long history of migration [Vargas-Silva *et al.*, 2009]. Five of the top 10 remittance-receiving countries are Asian, namely, Bangladesh, China, India, the Philippines, and Vietnam (*ibid.*). In 2011, remittances flowing to countries in Asia and the Pacific region reached US$204 billion, which was about 55% of the global total [Imai *et al.*, 2012]. As such, remittances have become an increasingly important source of income and are thought to have contributed to economic development in Asian countries [Siddique *et al.*, 2010; Jawaid and Raza, 2014]. A comprehensive investigation of the relationship of remittances to economic growth in Asia is therefore crucial for the understanding of this issue.

However, to the best of our knowledge, few studies examine the dynamic long-run impacts of remittances on economic growth in Asian countries. Moreover, few studies investigate whether these impacts depend on trade openness. In this study, we use panel data for 16 Asian countries over the period 1985–2011 to provide empirical evidence for the debate about the impacts of remittances on growth. From the dynamic estimation, we find that remittances have long-run significant positive impacts on growth with diminishing marginal effect. Positive impacts indeed depend on trade openness and decrease with increasing trade openness.

The remainder of this chapter is organized as follows. Section 4.2 summarizes previous studies on remittance flows to developing countries. Section 4.3 introduces the empirical approach applied in this study. Section 4.4 describes the data used. Section 4.5 outlines the empirical results. Section 4.6 concludes the analysis.

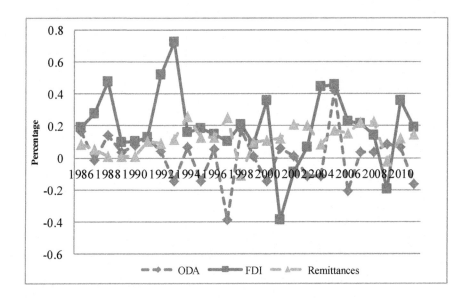

Figure 4.1. Growth Rates of ODA, FDI, and Remittances in 16 Asian Countries, 1986–2011.

Notes: The lists of 16 Asian countries are Bangladesh, Cambodia, China, Hong Kong, India, Indonesia, Israel, Jordan, Kazakhstan, Kyrgyzstan, Oman, Pakistan, the Philippines, South Korea, Sri Lanka, and Thailand. Remittances are the sum of inflows of workers' remittances, compensation of employees, and migrants' transfers.
Sources: Authors' depiction of data from World Bank [2011, 2014].

4.2 Literature Review

Remittances appear to make important contributions to Gross Domestic Product (GDP). Chami *et al.* [2008] point out that migrants' average remittances–GDP ratio was 3.6% for all developing countries during the period 1995–2004. On a country-by-country basis during the same period, the average remittances–GDP ratio exceeded 1% for over 60 countries, seven of which had an average ratio of 15% or higher [Barajas *et al.*, 2009]. United Nations [2011] notes that shares of remittances in GDP have grown for many developing countries, with remittances contributing more than 20% of GDP in some cases. Large remittances–GDP ratios indicate that remittances have great potential influence in developing countries. The US Department of State also suggests that remittances play an important role in promoting economic growth [Barajas *et al.*, 2009].

Yet, controversy about the empirical relationship between remittances and economic growth exists. Previous studies generally find that remittances have positive impacts on growth. These include Faini [2006], Giuliano and Ruiz-Arranz [2009], Fayissa and Nsiah [2010], Azam and Khan [2011], Das and Chowdhury [2011], Cooray [2012], Imai *et al.* [2012], Javid *et al.* [2012], Yaseen [2012], Dilshad [2013], Driffield and Jones [2013], Ukeje and Obiechina [2013], Jawaid and Raza [2014], and Kumar and Stauvermann [2014]. The positive impacts are increased production by stimulating consumption, acceleration of investment, reduction of regulations, and enhancement of human development by financing better health care and education [Barajas *et al.*, 2009; Calero, 2009; Gupta *et al.*, 2009; Javid *et al.*, 2012].

Other empirical studies find negative impacts of remittances on economic growth. These include Chami *et al.* [2003], Waheed and Aleem [2008], Karagöz [2009], and Jawaid and Raza [2012]. For example, Chami *et al.* [2003] point out that remittance inflows can reduce labor force participation and work efforts, thus reducing economic output. Further research to clearly outline the impacts of remittances on growth is evidently required.

For Asian countries, Cooray [2012] uses Ordinary Least Squares (OLS) and General Method of Moments (GMM) to investigate the impacts of migrants' remittances on growth in South Asia and finds positive and statistically significant impacts on education and financial sector development.

Imai *et al.* [2012] re-examine the impacts of remittances on GDP per capita growth for 24 countries in Asia and the Pacific region and confirm the positive impacts of remittances on economic growth, but highlight the adverse effect of remittance volatility on growth. This adverse effect is also supported by Jawaid and Raza [2014], who find that remittance volatility has negative impacts on growth in five Asian countries, Bangladesh, India, Nepal, Pakistan, and Sri Lanka, though the negative impact is not significant in Pakistan. They also examine the impact of remittances on growth in these five countries by applying the cointegration method. Their results indicate that there are significant positive long-run relationships between remittances and growth in Bangladesh, India, Nepal, and Sri Lanka, while there is a significant negative relationship in Pakistan.

Siddique *et al.* [2010], Javid *et al.* [2012], and Dilshad [2013] generate different results. By employing the Granger causality test, Siddique *et al.* [2010] find that growth in remittances leads to economic growth in Bangladesh and India but not in Sri Lanka. Javid *et al.* [2012] and Dilshad [2013] find significant positive impacts of remittances on growth in Pakistan by using the Autoregressive Distributed Lag (ARDL) approach and the OLS estimator, respectively.

Azam and Khan [2011] use the OLS estimator to investigate the impacts of remittances on growth in Armenia and Azerbaijan and find positive and significant effects. Karagöz [2009] uses the same estimator and finds a negative and significant impact of remittances on growth in Turkey.

Employing the error correction method and causality method, Jawaid and Raza [2012] examine the effects of remittances on growth in China and South Korea and find a long-run positive and significant impact in the latter, but a significant negative long-run relationship in the former.

4.3 The Autoregressive Distributed Lag (ARDL) Approach

To examine the long-run effects of remittances on economic growth, it is common to estimate the following static cross-sectional regression, as is done in studies by Vargas-Silva *et al.* [2009] and Driffield and Jones [2013]:

$$economic\ growth_{it} = \beta_0 + \beta_1 remittances_{it} + \omega control_{it} + \varepsilon_{it} \quad (4.1)$$

where *economic growth*$_{it}$ is the level of economic growth in period *t* for country *i*, *remittances*$_{it}$ is the index of remittance levels, *controls*$_{it}$ is a set of control variables, and ε_{it} is the error term. The static analysis in this estimation, however, suffers from endogeneity issues [Catrinescu *et al.*, 2009].

As Fayissa and Nsiah [2008], and Barguellil *et al.* [2013] suggest, the dynamic panel approach could address the endogenous problem, as well as capture economic growth adjustment dynamics and accommodate the persistence of remittance adjustments. Therefore, this study assesses the dynamic impacts of remittances on growth using dynamic panel econometric techniques. By using the dynamic panel model and including individual specific effects, we can control for heterogeneity in the dynamic relationship between remittances and growth across countries. One popular method to estimate the dynamic panel model is GMM, which was developed by Arellano and Bond [1991], and Arellano and Bover [1995]. Fayissa and Nsiah [2008], and Barguellil *et al.* [2013] use the GMM estimator to examine the dynamic effects of remittances on growth.

Two other approaches, the mean group (MG) and pooled mean group (PMG), can also estimate the dynamic panel model that encompasses both short- and long-run effects of remittances on economic growth. The PMG estimator, introduced by Pesaran *et al.* [1999], assumes that short-run coefficients and intercepts are heterogeneous while restricting long-run coefficients to being homogenous across countries. The MG estimator, introduced by Pesaran and Smith [1995], notably does not impose a homogeneity restriction on the long-run relationship between variables. Pesaran *et al.* [1999] point out that PMG estimators are consistent and asymptotically normal regardless of whether the regressors are I(0) or I(1). Compared to the MG estimator, the PMG estimator generates more efficient estimates if the homogeneity restrictions imposed by the method are valid [Koetter and Poghosyan, 2010]. The Hausman test, introduced in 1978, is used to test the results of PMG and MG estimators [Hausman, 1978].

In this study, we apply the PMG estimator to analyze the long-run dynamic effects of remittances on economic growth(eg) using a panel of 16 countries. The estimation procedure for the PMG estimator can briefly be described as follows. Suppose that the dynamic relationship between remittances and growth is given by the following ARDL (*p*, *q*,...,*q*) model, where the dependent and independent variables enter the right-hand side with lags of order *p* and *q*, respectively:

$$y_{it} = \sum_{j=1}^{p} \lambda_{ij} y_{i,t-j} + \sum_{j=0}^{q} \gamma'_{ij} x_{i,t-j} + \mu_i + \varepsilon_{it} \qquad (4.2)$$

where $i = 1, 2, ..., N$ is a country index, $t = 1, 2, ..., T$ is a time index (at the annual frequency), j is the number of time lags, $y_{it} = eg_{it}$, $x_{it} = (remittances_{it}, controls_{it})$, and μ_i are the fixed effects, λ_{ij} and γ_{ij} are the coefficients, and ε_{it} is a time-varying disturbance.

Eq. (4.2) can be re-parameterized as an error-correction form:

$$\Delta y_{it} = \phi_i (y_{i,t-1} - \theta'_i x_{i,t}) + \sum_{j=1}^{p-1} \lambda_{ij}^* \Delta y_{i,t-j} + \sum_{j=0}^{q-1} \gamma_{ij}'^* \Delta x_{i,t-j} + \mu_i + \varepsilon_{it} \qquad (4.3)$$

where $\phi_i = -(1 - \sum_{j=1}^{p} \lambda_{ij})$ gives the coefficients on error correction terms and measures the speed of adjustment of y_{it} toward its long-run equilibrium following a change in x_{it}; $\theta_i = \sum_{j=0}^{q} \gamma_{ij} / (1 - \sum_{j=1}^{p} \lambda_{ij})$ are the long-run coefficients; $\lambda_{ij}^* = -\sum_{m=j+1}^{p} \lambda_{im}$ ($j = 1, 2, ..., p-1$) and $\gamma_{ij}^* = -\sum_{m=j+1}^{q} \gamma_{im}$ ($j = 1, 2, ..., q-1$) are the short-run coefficients relating economic growth to its past values and other determinants, x_{it}. The MG estimator provides the averaged coefficients of individual time-series regressions for each country in the panel; this indicates that all the individual regressors are heterogeneous. However, the PMG estimator restricts the long-run coefficients, θ'_i; this is common across all regions. The error-correction speed of adjustment parameter ϕ_i and the short-run adjustment coefficients λ_{ij}^* and γ_{ij}^* vary across all regions. The speed of adjustment parameter ϕ_i should be negative; this is treated as evidence of cointegration between dependent and independent variables and would indicate the tendency of economic growth to return to its long-run equilibrium level [Kim *et al.*, 2010]. Once the estimates of short-run coefficients for individual countries are obtained, we can consistently estimate the cross-region mean of these parameters as

$$\lambda_j^* = \sum_{i=1}^{N} \lambda_{ij}^* / N \qquad j = 1, 2, ..., p - 1 \tag{4.4}$$

$$\gamma_j^* = \sum_{i=1}^{N} \gamma_{ij}^* / N \qquad j = 0, 1, ..., q - 1 \tag{4.5}$$

where N represents the number of regions.

4.4 Data

Given data availability, our dataset consists of a panel of 16 Asian countries with annual data over the period 1985–2011. Relevant terms and definitions are presented in Table 4.1.

Economic growth is measured by the annual percentage growth rates of GDP tracked by World Bank [2014][a]. Since Barguellil *et al.* [2013] conclude that remittances have effects on economic growth in countries with the largest remittances–GDP ratios and these effects disappear for countries with the highest levels of remittances, we use remittances–GDP ratios to compile the index of remittance levels. Remittances–GDP ratios represent the shares of remittances in GDP complied by Vargas-Silva *et al.* [2009]. Remittances here are defined as the sum of inflows of workers' remittances[b], compensation of employees, and migrants'

---

[a] World Bank [2014] indicates "World Development Indicators provides a compilation of relevant, high-quality, and internationally comparable statistics about global development and the fight against poverty."

[b] World Bank [2011] indicates "Workers' remittances, as defined by the International Monetary Fund (IMF) in the Balance of Payments manual, are current private transfers

transfers, and the data of remittances can be taken from World Bank [2011].

Table 4.1. Terms, sources, and definitions.

	Source	Definition
Remittances	World Bank [2011, 2014]	Share of remittances in GDP (%). Remittances are the sum of inflows of workers' remittances, compensation of employees, and migrants' transfers.
Economic growth	World Bank [2014]	Annual percentage growth rate of GDP (%).
Investment	World Bank [2014]	Annual growth rate of gross capital formation (%). This is the new investment in fixed capital assets in a county for a given year.
Openness	World Bank [2014]	Exports and imports as share of GDP (%).
Inflation	World Bank [2014]	Percentage change in the GDP deflator (%).

To strengthen our empirical results, we include other main control variables when analyzing the relationship between remittances and growth. Following Fayissa and Nsiah [2008], Vargas-Silva *et al.* [2009], Javid *et al.* [2012], Yaseen [2012], Barguellil *et al.* [2013], and Driffield and Jones [2013], these control variables include investment, trade openness, and inflation. Investment is measured by the annual growth rate of gross capital formation, which is expected to be positively related with economic growth. The index of trade openness levels uses the ratio of the sum of exports plus imports of goods to GDP. As stated by Manni *et al.* [2012] and Barguellil *et al.* [2013], greater trade openness leads to higher economic growth. The inflation rate is measured by the annual percent change in the GDP deflator. Many researchers, such as Cozier and Selody [1992], Motley [1994], and Barro [2013], find a negative

---

from migrant workers who are considered residents of the host country to recipients in the workers' country of origin."

relationship between inflation and economic growth. Hence, inflation is expected to negatively affect growth. Related investment, trade openness, and inflation data are collected from World Bank [2014]. A statistical description of the data is presented in Table 4.2.

Table 4.2. Statistical description of data.

Variable	Mean	Std. Dev.	Min.	Max.	Observations
Remittances	3.93	5.66	0.012	27.57	448
Economic growth	5.11	4.54	−20.10	18.70	411
Investment	6.27	14.99	−61.30	87.77	387
Openness	91.99	71.51	12.00	447.00	412
Inflation	23.35	133.28	−8.60	1546.70	414

4.5 Empirical Results

Before our actual estimation, we confirm the lags of all variables first. As Loayza and Ranciere [2006] suggest, we can impose a common lag structure across countries if we are mainly interested in the long-run effects of remittances on economic growth. The maximum lag of one is chosen for all variables to preserve the degrees of freedom while allowing for reasonably rich dynamics, which is consistent with previous studies that use the dynamic panel GMM model with the specification of one lag for dependent variables, such as Fayissa and Nsiah [2008], Imai *et al.* [2012], and Barguellil *et al.* [2013].

Following Vargas-Silva *et al.* [2009], we consider the square of remittances for diminishing returns. Table 4.3 shows the empirical results of PMG and MG estimators with and without the square of remittances. The upper part of Table 4.3 shows the common long-run coefficients, whereas the lower part shows the averaged short-run coefficients of all individual countries. The p-values of the Hausman test are over 10%. This indicates that the null hypothesis of homogeneous long-run coefficients for all parameters and all individuals should be accepted. Thus, PMG estimators are preferred. We should then focus on the empirical results of PMG estimators.

The average speed of adjustment coefficient (error correction coefficient) is negative and statistically significant, indicating the existence of a long-run relationship between remittances and growth. This finding also provides evidence of an adjustment of growth to the long-run equilibrium. The magnitude of the error correction coefficient reveals the speed of adjustment to the long-run equilibrium. For example, in Case 1, approximately 39% of the disequilibrium adjusts during a one-year interval. The half-life of a shock approximated by the ratio $-ln(2)/ln(1+\bar{\phi}_i)$ is about 1.29 years. The positive and significant long-run coefficients for remittances indicate that higher remittance levels promote economic growth in the long run. In a given year, a 1% increase in remittances as a share of GDP leads to a 0.19% increase in growth. By increasing savings, consumption, and investment, remittances lead to positive growth. This result is supported by previous studies such as Vargas-Silva *et al.* [2009], Imai *et al.* [2012], Yaseen [2012], and Driffield and Jones [2013].

With regard to the other main control variables, the long-run coefficients of investment and openness are positive and significant. This indicates that more investment and greater openness are associated with higher growth in the long run. For example, in Case 1, 1% increases in investment and openness lead to approximately 0.21% and 0.04% increases in economic growth, respectively. The negative and significant long-run coefficients of inflation indicate that higher inflation reduces growth, which is consistent with Barro [2013].

Compared to Case 1, Case 3 includes the square of remittances, whose coefficients are negative and significant. Therefore, we conclude that remittances have a positive but diminishing marginal effect on economic growth, which is consistent with the results of Vargas-Silva *et al.* [2009].

Table 4.3. Effects of remittances on economic growth (1)

Variable	PMG	MG	PMG	MG
	Case 1	Case 2	Case 3	Case 4
Long-run coefficients				
Remittances	0.1851***	4.4846*	0.6320***	25.5952
	(0.0616)	(2.6930)	(0.1019)	(18.8981)
(Remittances)^2			−0.0324***	−62.3588
			(0.0068)	(57.7328)
Investment	0.2139***	0.1182*	0.1709***	0.0978
	(0.0263)	(0.0604)	(0.0279)	(0.0824)
Openness	0.0418***	0.0385*	0.0368***	0.0313
	(0.0034)	(0.0207)	(0.0036)	(0.0298)
Inflation	−0.0255***	0.0612	−0.0260***	0.0347
	(0.0055)	(0.0930)	(0.0040)	(0.1139)
Error correction	−0.4146***	−0.7697***	−0.4132***	−0.9143***
	(0.0906)	(0.0724)	(0.0901)	(0.1336)
Short-run coefficients				
Δ Remittances	0.1332	−1.3015	10.6916	4.4663
	(1.1335)	(1.2538)	(8.5088)	(17.1838)
Δ (Remittances)^2			−33.2046	−50.5071
			(30.6949)	(61.7850)
Δ Investment	0.0438*	0.0184	0.0491**	−0.0335
	(0.0231)	(0.0275)	(0.0228)	(0.0466)
Δ Openness	−0.0035	−0.0548	−0.0342	0.0592
	(0.0284)	(0.0357)	(0.0503)	(0.1446)
Δ Inflation	−0.1373***	−0.0359	−0.1490***	0.0667
	(0.0385)	(0.0677)	(0.0404)	(0.0559)
Hausman Chi(2)	1.6078		4.1013	
p-value	0.8074		0.5349	

Notes: The dependent variable is economic growth. The Hausman test compares the PMG versus MG estimates under the null hypothesis that long-run coefficients are homogeneous for all parameters and individuals. If the null hypothesis is accepted, a PMG model is preferred. The values in the parentheses are the standard errors of corresponding coefficient estimates. ***, **, and * indicate statistical significance at 1%, 5%, and 10% levels, respectively.

Catrinescu *et al.* [2009] suggest that socio-economic conditions are an important variable affecting remittances' effects on economic growth. Trade openness is an important proxy for socio-economic conditions. To further explore whether the effects of remittances on growth depend on the level of trade openness, we interact remittances with trade openness. Table 4.4 shows the empirical results of remittances' effects on growth including interaction terms.

Again, the results of the Hausman test suggest the use of PMG estimators. Concerning Case 5 and Case 7, we find negative and significant error correction coefficients. These indicate the existence of long-run relationships between remittances and growth. The long-run coefficients of remittances on economic growth (0.5055 in Case 5 and 0.5098 in Case 7) indicate that remittances positively affect growth in the long run, which is robust with the results in Table 4.3. The long-run coefficients of investment, openness, and inflation all have the expected signs and are significant, which is consistent with the results shown in Table 4.3.

Notably, the long-run coefficients of interaction terms between remittances and openness are negative and significant. This indicates that the positive effects of remittances on growth decrease with greater trade openness. In other words, the positive effects of remittances on growth are less important in more open countries than in less open countries. Driffield and Jones [2013] demonstrate that remittances are relatively more important in the world's poorest countries. In general, greater trade openness helps the populations of countries become richer. Therefore, families in countries with greater openness are wealthy enough to live with fewer remittances, and hence, the importance and positive effects of remittances decrease.

Table 4.4. Effects of remittances on economic growth (2)

Variable	PMG	MG	PMG	MG
	Case 5	Case 6	Case 7	Case 8
Long-run coefficients				
Remittances	0.5055***	27.3307	0.5098***	−38.6755
	(0.0677)	(25.1490)	(0.0745)	(45.5395)
(Remittances)^2			−0.0009	544.9914
			(0.0074)	(555.3853)
Investment	0.2481***	0.1039	0.2411***	0.0657
	(0.0225)	(0.0637)	(0.0230)	(0.1354)
Openness	0.0405***	0.0779***	0.0395***	0.0965
	(0.0032)	(0.0231)	(0.0039)	(0.0698)
Remittances×Openness	−0.0048***	−0.1158	−0.0047***	−0.1945
	(0.0008)	(0.0864)	(0.0012)	(0.2758)
Inflation	−0.0257***	0.0520	−0.0221***	0.2111
	(0.0055)	(0.1439)	(0.0052)	(0.3376)
Error correction	−0.4745***	−1.9648*	−0.4540***	−0.9196***
	(0.0866)	(1.0872)	(0.0875)	(0.1254)
Short-run coefficients				
Δ Remittances	−33.7959	−1.3214	−13.4031	38.2102
	(29.6453)	(42.3548)	(22.7668)	(43.6179)
Δ (Remittances)^2			−90.6515	−240.0000
			(84.7370)	(249.1136)
Δ Investment	0.0269	−0.0427	0.0274	−0.0450
	(0.0250)	(0.0446)	(0.0253)	(0.0525)
Δ Openness	0.0509	−0.4494	0.0327	0.1188
	(0.0652)	(0.4005)	(0.0825)	(0.2285)
Δ Remittances×Openness	0.1058	0.8565	0.1074	−0.0095
	(0.1134)	(0.9122)	(0.1499)	(0.1294)
Δ Inflation	−0.1400***	−0.0670	−0.1431***	0.1019*
	(0.0361)	(0.0768)	(0.0425)	(0.0617)
Hausman Chi(2)	5.5656		0.3395	
p-value	0.3508		0.9871	

Note: Same as the notes of Table 4.3.

4.6 Conclusions

Given the apparent importance of remittances in determining economic growth, a growing body of literature has been examining the impacts of remittances on growth. Still, the relationship between remittances and growth remains unclear. Ambiguity may arise from the dual role of remittances: they tend to finance consumption and investment, which increases growth, but they can reduce labor force participation and work efforts, which decreases growth (though these are more short-term phenomena). Hence, to clearly understand the impacts of remittances on growth, it is necessary to distinguish the long-run effects from the short-run dynamics.

To shed light on this issue, we use the PMG estimator developed by Pesaran *et al.* [1999] to investigate the dynamic relationship between remittances and economic growth. This approach is particularly useful when long-run effects are expected to be homogeneous across countries while short-run adjustments depend on country characteristics, such as the level of financial development and socio-economic conditions. Moreover, we consider the impact of the square of remittances on economic growth, which allows us to estimate the marginal effect of remittances on growth. In addition, in order to explore whether impacts of remittances on economic growth depend on the level of trade openness, we interact remittances with trade openness.

Our results, which span 16 Asian countries over the period 1985–2011, show that the long-run coefficients of remittances are positive and statistically significant, indicating that remittances promote growth over the long term. The long-run coefficients of the square of remittances are negative and significant, indicating that the marginal effect of remittances on growth diminishes over the long term. In addition, the long-run coefficients of interaction terms between remittances and trade openness are negative and significant, indicating that the positive impacts of remittances on growth decrease with increasing trade openness. Thus, policy-makers in the selected Asian countries should formulate soft policies for workers' remittances and favorable policies to guide received remittances into productive sectors.

References

Arellano, M. and Bond, S. (1991). Some tests of specification for panel data: Monte Carlo evidence and an application to employment equations, *Review of Economic Studies*, 58, pp.277–297.

Arellano, M. and Bover, O. (1995). Another look at the instrumental variable estimation of error-components models, *Journal of Econometrics*, 68, pp.29–51.

Azam, M. and Khan, A. (2011). Workers' remittances and economic growth: Evidence from Azerbaijan and Armenia, *Global Journal of Human Social Science*, 11, pp.40–46.

Barajas, A., Chami, R., Fullenkamp, C., Gapen, M. and Montiel, P. (2009). Do workers' remittances promote economic growth? IMF Working Paper, WP/09/153.

Barguellil, A., Zaiem, M.H. and Zmami, M. (2013). Remittances, education and economic growth: A panel data analysis, *Journal of Business Studies Quarterly*, 4, pp.129–139.

Barro, R.J. (2013). Inflation and economic growth, *Annals of Economics and Finance*, 14, pp.121–144.

Calero, C. (2009). Remittances, liquidity constraints and human capital investments in Ecuador, *World Development*, 37, pp.1143–1154.

Catrinescu, N., Leon-Ledesma, M., Piracha, M. and Quillin, B. (2009). Remittances, institutions, and economic growth, *World Development*, 37, pp.81–92.

Chami, R., Barajas, A., Cosimano, T., Fullenkamp, C., Gapen, M. and Montiel, P. (2008). Macroeconomic consequences of remittances, IMF Occasional Paper, 259.

Chami, R., Fullenkamp, C. and Jahjah, S. (2003). Are immigrant remittance flows a source of capital for development? IMF Working Paper, WP/03/189.

Cooray, A.V. (2012). The impact of migrant remittances on economic growth: Evidence from South Asia, *Review of International Economics*, 20, pp.985–998.

Cozier, B. and Selody, J. (1992). Inflation and macroeconomic performance: Some cross-country evidence, Bank of Canada Working Paper, No. 06.

Das, A. and Chowdhury, M. (2011). Remittances and GDP dynamics in 11 developing countries: Evidence from panel cointegration and PMG techniques, *Romanian Economic Journal*, 14, pp.3–24.

Dilshad, W.B. (2013). Impact of workers' remittances on economic growth: An empirical study of Pakistan's economy, *International Journal of Business and Management*, 8, pp.126–131.

Driffield, N. and Jones, C. (2013). Impact of FDI, ODA and migrant remittances on economic growth in developing countries: A systems approach, *European Journal of Development Research*, 25, pp.173–196.

Faini, R. (2006). Migration and remittance: The impact on the countries of origin. Paper presented at the Fourth AFD/EUDN Conference on "Migration and Development: Mutual Benefits?" November Paris.

Fayissa, B. and Nsiah, C. (2008). The impact of remittances on economic growth and development in Africa, Middle Tennessee State University Working Paper Series, February.

Fayissa, B. and Nsiah, C. (2010). Can remittances spur economic growth and development? Evidence from Latin American Countries (LACs), Middle Tennessee State University Working Paper Series, March.

Giuliano, P. and Ruiz-Arranz, M. (2009). Remittances, financial development, and growth, *Journal of Development Economics*, 90, pp.144–152.

Gupta, S., Pattillo, C.A. and Wagh, S. (2009). Effect of remittances on poverty and financial development in Sub-Saharan Africa, *World Development*, 37, pp.104–115.

Hausman, J.A. (1978). Specification tests in econometrics, *Econometrica*, 46, pp.1251–1371.

Imai, K.S., Gaiha, R., Ali, A. and Kaicker, N. (2012). Remittances, growth and poverty: New evidence from Asian countries, International Fund for Agricultural Development Occasional Papers, 15.

Javid, M., Arif, U. and Qayyum, A. (2012). Impact of remittances on economic growth and poverty, *Academic Research International*, 2, pp.433–447.

Jawaid, S.T. and Raza, S.A. (2012). Workers' remittances and economic growth in China and Korea: An empirical analysis, *Journal of Chinese Economic and Foreign Trade Studies*, 5, pp.185–193.

Jawaid, S.T. and Raza, S.A. (2014). Effects of workers' remittances and its volatility on economic growth in South Asia, *International Migration*, doi: 10.1111/imig.12151.

Karagöz, K. (2009). Workers' remittances and economic growth: Evidence from Turkey, *Journal of Yasar University*, 4, pp.1891–1908.

Kim, D-H., Lin, S-C. and Suen, Y-B. (2010). Dynamic effects of trade openness on financial development, *Economic Modelling*, 27, pp.254–261.

Koetter, M. and Poghosyan, T. (2010). Real estate prices and bank stability, *Journal of Banking and Finance*, 34, pp.1129–1138.

Kumar, R.R. and Stauvermann, P.J. (2014). Exploring the effects of remittances on Lithuanian economic growth, *Inzinerine Ekonomika-Engineering Economics*, 25, pp.250–260.

Loayza, N. and Ranciere, R. (2006). Financial development, financial fragility, and growth, *Journal of Money, Credit and Banking*, 38, pp.1051–1076.

Manni, U.H., Siddiqui, S.A. and Afzal, M.N.I. (2012). An empirical investigation on trade openness and economic growth in Bangladesh economy, *Asian Social Science*, 8, pp.154–159.

Motley, B. (1994). Growth and inflation: A cross-country study, Federal Reserve Bank of San Francisco Working Paper, pp.94–108.

Pesaran, M.H. and Smith, R. (1995). Estimating long-run relationships from dynamic heterogeneous panels, *Journal of Econometrics*, 68, pp.79–113.

Pesaran, M.H., Shin, Y. and Smith, R.P. (1999). Pooled mean group estimation of dynamic heterogeneous panels, *Journal of the American Statistical Association*, 94, pp.621–634.

Ratha, D., Mohapatra, S. and Silwal, A. (2009). Migration and remittance trends 2009, World Bank Migration and Development Brief, 11.

Siddique, A., Selvanathan, E.A. and Selvanathan, S. (2010). Remittances and economic growth: Empirical evidence from Bangladesh, India and Sri Lanka, University of Western Australia Discussion Paper, 10.27.

Ukeje, E.U. and Obiechina, M.E. (2013). Workers' remittances– economic growth nexus: Evidence from Nigeria, using an error correction methodology, *International Journal of Humanities and Social Science*, 3, pp. 212–227.

United Nations (2011). Impact of remittances on poverty in developing countries. United Nations Conference on Trade and Development, UNCTAD/DITC/TNCD/2010/8.

Vargas-Silva, C., Jha, S. and Sugiyarto, G. (2009). Remittances in Asia: Implications for the fight against poverty and the pursuit of economic growth, ADB Economics Working Paper Series, 182.

Waheed, A. and Aleem, A. (2008). Workers' remittances and economic growth: Empirical evidence from Pakistan, *Journal of Social Science and Humanities*, 47, pp.1–12.

Wakayama, Y. (2011). Can remittances be the source of GDP growth in the developing countries? Analyzing remittances in ECA countries, Tokyo University of Foreign Studies, Bachelor Thesis.

World Bank (2011). Migration and Remittances Factbook 2011, World Bank, Washington, D.C.

World Bank (2014). World Development Indicators 2014, World Bank, Washington, D.C.

Yaseen, H.S. (2012). The positive and negative impact of remittances on economic growth in MENA countries, *Journal of International Management Studies*, 7, pp.7–14.

Chapter 5

Effects of Remittances on Poverty Reduction in Asia

Takeshi Inoue
Faculty of Policy Studies, Nanzan University
Seirei-Cho, Seto 489-0863, Japan
Email: tinoue@ps.nanzan-u.ac.jp

Shigeyuki Hamori
Faculty of Economics, Kobe University
2-1, Rokkodai, Nada-Ku, Kobe 657-8501, Japan
Email: hamori@econ.kobe-u.ac.jp

5.1 Introduction

Developing countries have significantly reduced extreme poverty during the last two decades. According to the World Bank, the number of extremely poor people living on less than US$1.25 per day at 2005 purchasing power parity (PPP) prices declined from 1.92 billion people (36.4% of the global population) in 1990 to 1.01 billion people (14.5%) in 2011 (Figures 5.1 and 5.2). Therefore, the international target of reducing the number of people living in extreme poverty by half between 1990 and 2015 had been achieved—five years ahead of the deadline.

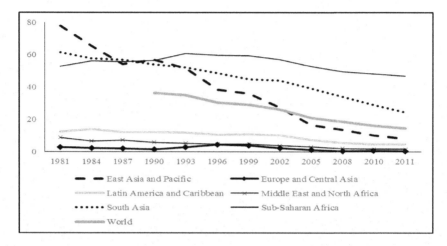

Figure 5.1. Percentage of population below the International Poverty Line (% of population).
Sources: World Bank [2014].

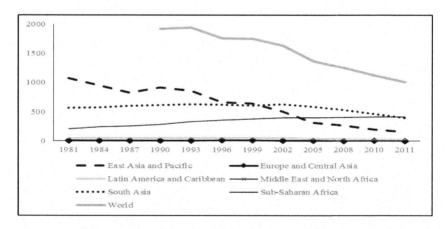

Figure 5.2. Number of population below the International Poverty Line (numbers in million).
Sources: World Bank [2014].

This was mainly realized through rapid economic growth and the accompanying poverty reduction in Asia.

As such, since the 1980s, Asia has attracted attention as a region of growth and poverty reduction among developing countries. Recently, Asia has also gained recognition as a region comprising countries that are the top recipients of remittances. Official remittances have grown significantly in volume since the beginning of the 2000s, thus enhancing the importance of external sources of finance for economic growth. The regional breakdown indicates that South Asia and East Asia Pacific have received the largest amount of official remittances since the mid-2000s; these regions have led the significant growth in remittance inflows into developing countries (Figure 5.3). This surge in cross-border capital flows is expected to have influenced the economies of recipient countries.

For example, migrants' remittances may help their family members in their home country to obtain additional income and thus enable them to expand their consumption, promote physical and human capital accumulation, and increase financial investments [IMF, 2005, p.72]. Accordingly, an increase in remittances is expected to stimulate economic growth and reduce poverty in remittance-receiving countries.

In contrast, remittances are also considered to have a detrimental effect on economic growth. This is because migrants' remittances are compensatory transfers and therefore countercyclical to the home country's economic condition [Chami *et al.*, 2005, p.56]. Moreover, as remittances may be used by the family members to reduce their participation in the local labor market, they would negatively affect economic activity in the home country [*ibid.*, p.77].

Empirically, previous studies featuring large samples of countries have generally indicated that international remittances indeed promote economic growth [Acosta *et al.*, 2008; Pradhan *et al.*, 2008; Catrinescu *et al.*, 2009; Giuliano and Ruiz-Arranz, 2009; Mundaca, 2009; Ramirez and Sharma, 2009; Bettin and Zazzaro, 2011] and alleviate poverty [Adams and Page, 2005; IMF, 2005; Acosta *et al.*, 2008; Gupta *et al.*, 2009; Portes, 2009]. However, to the best of our knowledge, few empirical studies have examined the impact of remittances on poverty reduction,

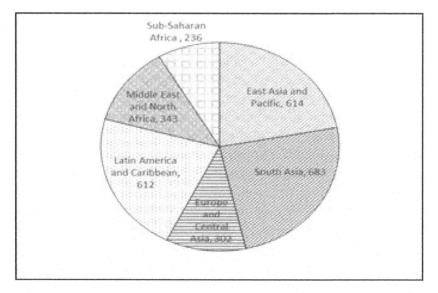

Figure 5.3. Remittance inflows to developing countries from 2000 to 2012 (amount in US$ billion).
Source: World Bank [2014].

especially in Asia. Therefore, we aim to contribute to the literature by elucidating this point.

The remainder of this chapter is organized as follows. Section 5.2 provides a review of related literature. In Section 5.3, we introduce the model, and in Section 5.4, we explain the definitions, sources, and properties of the data. We present the estimation results in Section 5.5, and summarize our main findings in Section 5.6.

5.2 Literature Review

As seen in the previous chapter of this book, many empirical studies have investigated the growth-promoting effect of remittances. Furthermore, empirical analyses have begun to examine the poverty-alleviating effect of remittances using multi-country data. In this section, we review previous studies related to the remittances-poverty nexus in developing countries[a].

One of the first studies concerning this topic was by Adams and Page [2005], who examined the impacts of official remittances on poverty conditions using data from 71 developing countries. In their model, the poverty indicator was explained by international remittances and control variables. Poverty conditions were measured by three different indicators—namely, the poverty headcount ratio, the poverty gap, and the squared poverty gap—whereas international remittances were defined as either the share of migrants in a country's population or the per capita international remittances received by a developing country. Using ordinary least squares (OLS) and instrumental variables estimations, they showed that international remittances have a negative, statistically significant impact on all three poverty indicators though the share of migrants has a negative, statistically significant impact only on the poverty ratio and poverty gap.

Similarly, Gupta *et al.* [2009] investigated the direct effect of remittances on poverty for 76 developing countries from 1980 to 2003. They estimated a system of equations where both poverty and remittances were endogenously determined by the three-stage least squares method. Their results indicated that remittances have a poverty-reducing effect and that the magnitude of this effect is similar to that of the OLS estimates conducted by them. However, the average poverty-reducing elasticity of remittances was consistently found to be smaller than the average remittance-inducing elasticity of poverty. Therefore, they indicated the possibility that the effect of poverty on out-migration and remittance inflows might be greater than the effect of remittances on poverty reduction.

Further, Vargas-Silva *et al.* [2009] analyzed whether remittances alleviated poverty conditions in developing Asian countries from 1988 to

---

[a] In addition, IMF [2005] and Portes [2009] are among the related empirical literature on the effect of remittances on poverty conditions. IMF [2005] revealed a strong relationship between poverty measures and remittances in 101 countries, both advanced and developing, whereas Portes [2009] suggested that remittances increase the income of the bottom 70 % of the population in low-income countries.

2007. They used three alternative measures of assessing poverty conditions: the poverty headcount ratio at the national poverty line, and the poverty headcount ratio and the poverty gap at US$1.25 per day at PPP prices. Fixed-effects and random-effects estimations indicated that the impact of remittances on poverty depends on the measure of poverty used and the methodology chosen. Specifically, based on their estimation results, they stated that remittances decrease the poverty gap, thereby ameliorating the depth of poverty, but that remittances have a negative but insignificant effect on the poverty ratio in Asia.

Finally, unlike the studies cited above, Acosta *et al.* [2008] used a panel dataset for 59 countries from 1970 to 2000 to explore the indirect impacts of remittances on poverty through income level and inequality. They specified a model in which per capita GDP growth or changes in the Gini coefficient depend on remittances, remittances interacted with a regional dummy for Latin American and Caribbean (LAC) countries, and control variables. The results of their system generalized method of moments estimation indicated that remittances cause income growth in typical countries worldwide as well as in an average LAC country. They also revealed that remittances tend to increase income inequality in typical countries worldwide, whereas they slightly reduce inequality or leave it unchanged in average LAC countries depending on the choice of instrument variables. Based on these results, they concluded that remittances would reduce poverty in the LAC countries.

As stated above, previous studies generally suggested that remittances tend to reduce poverty in developing countries. Herein, we analyze the poverty-reducing effect of remittances focusing on developing Asia, including its large-recipient countries.

5.3 Model

We conduct a panel analysis using annual data from the Asian region. The dependent variable is the poverty ratio. The model is defined as follows:

$$POV_{it} = \beta_o + \beta_1 REM_{it} + \gamma X_{it} + u_{it}, \quad i = 1, 2, \cdots, N : t = 1, 2, \cdots, T. \quad (5.1)$$

Here, POV_{it} is the poverty ratio in country i during time period t, REM_{it} represents the remittances in country i during time period t, X_{it} is the vector of control variables in country i during time period t, and u_{it} is the error term in country i during time period t. We use the following control variables: per capita GDP, financial development, the inflation rate, trade openness, and education level. Table 5.1 provides the definitions of the data; Table 5.2 presents the summary statistics for each data.

5.4 Data

We use annual panel data from 18 Asian countries from 1980 to 2012. The selected countries are from the East Asia Pacific region and South Asia and include countries classified as low-income, lower-middle-income, and upper-middle-income countries[b]. Data were obtained from the World Development Indicators (WDI) published by World Bank [2014].

5.4.1 *Dependent variable*

The poverty ratio (*POV*) is used as the dependent variable in this empirical analysis. This paper measures the poverty ratio as the poverty headcount ratio at US$1.25 per day (% of population).

5.4.2 *Explanatory variables*

Remittances
Remittances (*REM*) is the important explanatory variable focused on in this study. Remittances comprise the personal remittances received and are measured as a percentage of GDP. As an increase in migrants' remittances may help their family members obtain additional income and

---

[b] The 18 countries covered in this study are as follows: Bangladesh, Bhutan, Cambodia, China, Fiji, India, Indonesia, Laos, Malaysia, Maldives, Micronesia, Nepal, Pakistan, Papua New Guinea, the Philippines, Sri Lanka, Thailand, and Vietnam.

improve their standard of living, the coefficient of *REM* in Eq. (5.1) is
expected to be negative.

Table 5.1. Definition of data.

Variable	Definition
POV	Poverty headcount ratio at $1.25/day (PPP) (% of population)
REM	Personal remittances, received (% of GDP)
PGDP	Log of GDP per capita (constant 2005 US$)
M2	Money and quasi money (% of GDP)
CREDIT	Domestic credit to private sector by banks (% of GDP)
INF	Inflation, consumer prices (annual %)
OPEN	Exports and imports of goods and services (% of GDP)
SCL1	Primary school enrollment (% gross)
SCL2	Secondary school enrollment (% gross)
SCL3	Tertiary school enrollment (% gross)

Table 5.2. Summary statistics.

Variable	Mean	Standard Deviation
POV	30.812	22.066
REM	2.975	3.772
PGDP	6.789	0.869
M2	52.420	33.201
CREDIT	38.617	33.672
INF	8.100	9.234
OPEN	79.802	51.578
SCL1	101.832	23.179
SCL2	48.604	21.575
SCL3	11.549	11.169

Per capita GDP
Per capita GDP (*PGDP*) is the GDP per capita (in constant 2005 US dollars). Since an increase in per capita GDP may help poor people obtain more income, the coefficient of *PGDP* in Eq. (5.1) is expected to be negative.

Financial Development
To measure financial development, we use two proxy variables: money supply ($M2$) and domestic credit (*CREDIT*). $M2$ is the money and quasi money measured as a percentage of GDP. *CREDIT* is the domestic credit provided to the private sector by banks measured as a percentage of GDP. Here, credit refers to financial resources provided to the private sector by financial corporations. As an increase in financial development leads to increased economic activities among households and companies facing funding constraints, the coefficient of financial development in Eq. (5.1) may be negative[c].

Inflation Rate
We also consider the inflation rate (*INF*) as a control variable. *INF* is the inflation rate of consumer prices and is measured as an annual percentage. Easterly and Fischer [2001] found that high inflation tends to increase poverty. In line with the literature, we expect the coefficient of *INF* to be positive in Eq. (5.1).

Trade Openness
As a control variable, we use the indicator of trade openness, namely the ratio of imports and exports to GDP (*OPEN*). Hamori and Hashiguchi [2012] suggested that in poor countries, globalization benefits only those with basic and higher education and lowers the income share of those with no education; thus, the coefficient of *OPEN* in Eq. (5.1) is expected

---

[c] Several studies empirically indicate that financial development helps reduce poverty both directly and indirectly through its effect on economic growth [e.g., Honohan, 2004; Jalilian and Kirkpatrick, 2005; Beck *et al.*, 2007; Jeanneney and Kpodar, 2008; Quartey, 2008; Inoue and Hamori, 2012].

to be positive [see also Ravallion, 2001; Dollar and Kraay, 2002; Milanovic, 2005].

Education Level
We include three proxy variables to measure education level as a control variable: the primary school enrollment ratio (*SCL*1), the secondary school enrollment ratio (*SCL*2), and the tertiary school enrollment ratio (*SCL*3). As increased education levels foster human resource development and consequently poverty reduction, the coefficient of these variables in Eq. (5.1) is expected to be negative.

5.5 Results

The estimation results of Eq. (5.1) are divided into six cases—because we used two proxy variables for financial development and three proxy variables for education level—and are reported in Tables 5.3 and 5.4. Along with the estimated coefficients for the explanatory variables, the tables present their standard errors and *p*-values based on the redundant fixed-effects test and the Hausman test. These two tests facilitate the selection of a model to estimate the panel data.

The null hypothesis of the redundant fixed-effects test is that there is no unobserved heterogeneity, or in other words, no fixed effect; therefore, the fixed-effects model is chosen when the null hypothesis is rejected. As for the Hausman test, the null hypothesis is that the individual effects are uncorrelated with the other regressors in the model; therefore, the fixed-effects model is chosen when the null hypothesis is rejected. The results show that the null hypotheses are rejected at the 5% significance level in both tests. Therefore, we use the fixed-effects model to estimate Eq. (5.1).

Let us examine the results of Table 5.3, which indicate the empirical results using $M2$ as the proxy variable for financial development. The estimation results of the coefficients in Eq. (5.1) are as follows. First, the coefficients for remittances are negative, as expected, and statistically significant at the 5% level in all cases (−0.882 in Case 1, −0.989 in

Case 2, and −1.117 in Case 3). These results indicate that an increase in remittances will lead to poverty reduction.

Table 5.3. Empirical results (1).

Dependent Variable: Poverty ratio

	Case 1		Case 2		Case 3	
	Estimate	Standard Error	Estimate	Standard Error	Estimate	Standard Error
REM	−0.882	0.387**	−0.989	0.410**	−1.117	0.422***
PGDP	−32.356	4.049***	−26.524	5.831***	−32.679	5.433**
M2	−0.002	0.081	0.047	0.090	0.022	0.086
INF	0.026	0.146	0.025	0.174	−0.048	0.162
OPEN	0.142	0.054***	0.201	0.060***	0.189	0.068***
SCL1	−0.221	0.122*				
SCL2			−0.297	0.137**		
SCL3					−0.159	0.210
Sample Size	90		84		82	
Adjusted R²	0.868		0.870		0.863	
Redundant Fixed-effects Test (p-value)	8.012 (0.000)		7.632 (0.000)		6.146 (0.000)	
Hausman Test (p-value)	14.862 (0.021)		15.121 (0.019)		17.101 (0.009)	

Note: ***, **, and * indicate that the null hypothesis is rejected at the 1%, 5%, and 10% level, respectively.

Further, Table 5.3 shows the estimation results of the control variables, namely per capita GDP, financial development, the inflation rate, trade openness, and education level. The coefficients of per capita GDP in logarithms are estimated to be –32.356 in Case 1, –26.524 in Case 2, and –32.679 in Case 3. These results suggest that a rise in per capita GDP will lead to poverty reduction.

The coefficients of $M2$ are estimated to range from –0.002 to 0.047 and are not statistically significant. Similarly, the coefficients of the inflation rate are estimated to range from –0.048 to 0.026; they are not significant in any case. Therefore, money supply and the inflation rate do not seem to significantly influence the poverty ratio.

Next, the coefficients of trade openness are estimated to be positive (0.142 in Case 1, 0.201 in Case 2, and 0.189 in Case 3), and they are statistically significant. Thus, increased trade openness will lead to an increase in the poverty ratio. Hamori and Hashiguchi [2012] indicated that inequality increases with increasing values of the openness variable. Our results indicate that the poverty ratio increases with increasing values of the openness variable.

In terms of the effect of education, the coefficients of the primary school enrollment ratio ($SCL1$) and the secondary school enrollment ratio ($SCL2$) are estimated to be –0.221 and –0.297, respectively, and both are statistically significant. Therefore, increased education levels may decrease the poverty ratio.

Let us move to the empirical results shown in Table 5.4, which use *CREDIT* as the proxy variable for financial development. The estimation results of the coefficients in Eq. (5.1) are as follows. Empirically, results in Table 5.4 are consistent with those in Table 5.3. First, the coefficients of remittances are negative, as expected, and statistically significant at the 1% level in all cases (–0.906 in Case 4, –0.933 in Case 5, and –1.107 in Case 6). These results indicate that an increase in remittances will lead to poverty reduction.

Table 5.4 also displays the estimation results of the control variables. The coefficients of per capita GDP in logarithms are estimated to be –32.924 in Case 4, –24.822 in Case 5, and –32.567 in Case 6. These results suggest that a rise in per capita GDP will lead to poverty reduction.

The coefficients of *CREDIT* are estimated to be within the range of –0.001 and 0.024 and are not statistically significant. Similarly, the coefficients of the inflation rate are estimated to range from –0.052 to

0.028; they are not significant in any case. Therefore, financial development and the inflation rate do not seem to significantly influence the poverty ratio.

Next, the coefficients of trade openness are estimated to be positive (0.139 in Case 4, 0.207 in Case 5, and 0.187 in Case 6), and they are statistically significant. Thus, increased trade openness will lead to an increase in the poverty ratio.

Table 5.4. Empirical results (2).

Dependent Variable: Poverty ratio

	Case 4		Case 5		Case 6	
	Estimate	Standard Error	Estimate	Standard Error	Estimate	Standard Error
REM	−0.906	0.378**	−0.933	0.402**	−1.107	0.413***
PGDP	−32.924	3.165***	−24.822	5.429***	−32.567	4.789***
CREDIT	0.024	0.058	−0.001	0.063	0.023	0.067
INF	0.028	0.144	0.007	0.171	−0.052	0.160
OPEN	0.139	0.052***	0.207	0.060***	0.187	0.069***
SCL1	−0.219	0.121*				
SCL2			−0.298	0.142**		
SCL3					−0.142	0.217
Sample Size	90		84		82	
Adjusted R^2	0.868		0.870		0.863	
Redundant Fixed-effects Test (p-value)	8.168 (0.000)		7.705 (0.000)		6.182 (0.000)	
Hausman Test (p-value)	14.235 (0.027)		14.438 (0.025)		16.803 (0.010)	

Note: Same as the note of Table 5.3.

Lastly, the coefficients of the primary school enrollment ratio ($SCL1$) and the secondary school enrollment ratio ($SCL2$) are estimated to be − 0.219 and −0.298, respectively, and both are statistically significant. Therefore, increased education levels may decrease the poverty ratio.

To summarize, Tables 5.3 and 5.4 show that an increase in remittances has a decreasing effect on the poverty ratio. Further, an increase in real GDP or in primary or secondary education level will lead to a decrease in the poverty ratio, whereas increased trade openness leads to an increase in the poverty ratio. These results are robust for financial development variables. In contrast, financial development and inflation rate do not show significant effects on the poverty ratio.

5.6 Conclusions

Especially since the early 2000s, the Asian region has attracted the largest amount of migrants' remittances. In the 1990s, four of the world's top ten remittance-receiving countries were in Asia (India, the Philippines, China, and Pakistan). These countries accounted for approximately 34% of the total remittance inflows into the developing world. From 2000 until 2012, Bangladesh was included in this list, and the share of remittances into these five Asian countries increased to approximately 44%.

In this chapter, we empirically analyze whether and how the surging inflow of remittances influences poverty conditions in Asia. Using unbalanced panel data for 18 Asian countries from 1980 to 2012, we estimate the models in which the poverty headcount ratio is explained by remittances and certain control variables, namely per capita GDP, financial development (M2 or domestic credit), the inflation rate, trade openness, and education level (primary, secondary, or tertiary school enrollment ratio).

The empirical results indicate that remittance inflows have a negative and statistically significant effect on the poverty ratio, suggesting that remittances could be a useful instrument for poverty reduction in Asia. This evidence is robust to changes in the measures of financial development and education levels. Since the 1980s, extreme poverty in

Asia has significantly declined both in absolute terms and as a share of the total population; this has contributed to a worldwide reduction in poverty in the last few decades. Therefore, this finding implies that remittance inflows to Asia are among the driving forces of this phenomenon.

Moreover, we find that increases in per capita GDP and primary or secondary school enrollment ratio improve the poverty ratio, whereas increases in trade openness worsen poverty conditions. Though several studies argue that international openness stimulates economic growth [e.g., Dollar and Kraay, 2002], our results conversely suggest that international trade has a harmful effect on the poor. This is because poor people are unlikely to benefit from expanded export opportunities, whereas import expansion may deprive them of their necessities, which in turn would worsen their standard of living. Therefore, to promote further poverty reduction in Asia, the countries should promote remittance inflows, enhance education level, increase per capita income, and expand support for the poor who are adversely affected by trade openness.

References

Acosta, P., Calderón, C., Fajnzylber, P. and Lopez, H. (2008). What is the impact of international remittances on poverty and inequality in Latin America? *World Development*, 36, pp. 89–114.

Adams, R.H. Jr. and Page, J. (2005). Do international migration and remittances reduce poverty in developing countries? *World Development*, 33, pp. 1645–1669.

Beck, T., Demirgüç-Kunt, A. and Levine, R. (2007). Finance, inequality and the poor, *Journal of Economic Growth*, 12, pp. 27–49.

Bettin, G. and Zazzaro, A. (2011). Remittances and financial development: Substitutes or complements in economic growth, *Bulletin of Economic Research*, 64, pp. 509–536.

Catrinescu, N., Leon-Ledesma, M., Piracha, M. and Quillin, B. (2009). Remittances, institutions, and economic growth, *World Development*, 37, pp. 81–92.

Chami, R., Fullenkamp, C. and Jahjah, S. (2005). Are immigrant remittance flows a source of capital for development? IMF Staff Papers, 52, pp. 55–81.

Dollar, D. and Kraay, A. (2002). Growth is good for the poor, *Journal of Economic Growth*, 7, pp. 195–225.

Easterly, W. and Fischer, S. (2001). Inflation and the poor, *Journal of Money, Credit and Banking*, 33, pp. 160–178.

Giuliano, P. and Ruiz-Arranz, M. (2009). Remittances, financial development, and growth, *Journal of Development Economics*, 90, pp. 144–152.

Gupta, S., Pattillo, C.A. and Wagh, S. (2009). Effect of remittances on poverty and financial development in Sub-Saharan Africa, *World Development*, 37, pp. 104–115.

Hamori, S. and Hashiguchi, Y. (2012). The effect of financial deepening on inequality: Some international evidence, *Journal of Asian Economics*, 23, pp. 353–359.

Honohan, P. (2004). Financial development, growth and poverty: How close are the links? World Bank Policy Research Working Paper, 3203.

Inoue, T. and Hamori, S. (2012). How has financial deepening affected poverty reduction in India? Empirical analysis using state-level panel data, *Applied Financial Economics*, 22, pp. 395–408.

International Monetary Fund (IMF) (2005). World Economic Outlook April 2005: Globalization and External Imbalances, IMF, Washington, D.C.

Jalilian, H. and Kirkpatrick, C. (2005). Does financial development contribute to poverty reduction? *Journal of Development Studies*, 41, pp. 636–656.

Jeanneney, S.G. and Kpodar, K. (2008). Financial development and poverty reduction: Can there be a benefit without a cost? IMF Working Paper, WP/08/62.

Milanovic, B. (2005). Can we discern the effect of globalization on income distribution? Evidence from household survey, *World Bank Economic Review*, 19, pp. 21–44.

Mundaca, B.G. (2009). Remittances, financial market development, and economic growth: The case of Latin America and the Caribbean, *Review of Development Economics*, 13, pp. 288–303.

Portes, L.S.V. (2009). Remittances, poverty and inequality, *Journal of Economic Development*, 34, pp. 127–140.

Pradhan, G., Upadhyay, M. and Upadhyaya, K. (2008). Remittances and economic growth in developing countries, *The European Journal of Development Research*, 20, pp. 497–506.

Quartey, P. (2008). Financial sector development, savings mobilization and poverty reduction in Ghana, in *Financial Development, Institutions, Growth and Poverty Reduction*, Guha-Khasnobis, B. and Mavrotas, G. (eds.), pp. 87–119. Basingstoke: Palgrave Macmillan.

Ramirez, M.D. and Sharma, H. (2009). Remittances and growth in Latin America: A panel unit root and panel cointegration analysis, *Economic Studies of International Development*, 9, pp. 5–36.

Ravallion, M. (2001). Growth, inequality and poverty: Looking beyond averages, *World Development*, 29, pp. 1803–1815.

Vargas-Silva, C., Jha, S. and Sugiyarto, G. (2009). Remittances in Asia: Implications for the fight against poverty and the pursuit of economic growth, ADB Economics Working Paper Series, 182.

World Bank (2014). World Development Indicators 2014, World Bank, Washington, D.C.

Chapter 6

Financial Development and Growth in Resource-Rich Countries

Kazue Demachi

Graduate School of International Cooperation Studies, Kobe University

2-1, Rokkodai-cho, Nada-Ku, Kobe 657-8501 Hyogo, Japan

Email: k.demachi@people.kobe-u.ac.jp

Takuji Kinkyo

Faculty of Economics, Kobe University

2-1, Rokkodai-cho, Nada-Ku, Kobe, 657-8501 Hyogo, Japan

Email: kinkyo@econ.kobe-u.ac.jp

6.1 Introduction

Many studies have evaluated the effect of financial development on economic growth. King and Levine [1993], Levine [1997], Levin *et al.* [2000], and Demigüç-Kunt and Levine [2008], among others, have shown through econometric estimation that financial development has a

119

favorable impact on growth. In parallel, the direction of causality, namely, the endogeneity of financial development to economic growth, has been much discussed. The robustness of the theory on financial development has been examined in various ways, including the use of instrumental variables. The applicability of the theory to various countries has also been investigated [Levine and Renelt, 1992].

This chapter evaluates the effect of financial development on economic growth in countries that are rich in natural resources (hereafter "resource countries"). Since around the 2000s, many developing countries' economies started to grow due to foreign investments in development of natural gas, crude oil, and metals. In particular, resource-led growth of less developed countries occurred in Africa, which experienced stagnation in the 1980s and 1990s but regained strength in the 2000s, and in Latin America and Central Asia. In many East Asian countries, on the other hand, manufacturing and services are relatively developed; therefore, the economic diversification masks the importance of natural resources in their economies. However, approximately 30% of Malaysia's government budget depends on natural gas exported by its national gas company [Yusof, 2011], while low-income countries such as Laos and Myanmar depend on the inflow of foreign money from natural gas exports.

Development and export of natural resources are associated with massive capital flows into the domestic (and foreign) financial system of resource countries. The effects of financial development on growth in such countries are examined in this chapter. We have performed a generalized method of moments (GMM) analysis of panel data consists of 140 countries (at maximum) and five periods (25 years) from 1982 to 2006. While most of the related studies have focused on oil-exporting countries, we have included countries that export oil and countries that export other natural resources (natural gas and mining products), because "resource curse" problems are also seen in those countries.

6.2 Natural Resources and Growth

The relationship between economic growth and being a resource country has been analyzed and discussed from various perspectives. Sachs and Warner [1995; 2001] pointed out the negative correlation between primary exports and economic growth. The problems associated with structural changes in resource-exporting economies and the influence of changes in exchange ratio have been discussed under the name of Dutch disease [Corden, 1981; Corden and Neary, 1982; Corden, 1984]. The correlation between natural resource endowment and violent conflicts has also been debated [Collier and Hoeffler, 2001]. Those are cases in which natural resource abundance has turned out not to be "blessing" for the economy but rather a "curse." On this point, recent analysis seems to put more weight on the importance of institutions and their qualities. Several studies have presented a view that the "resource curse," economic stagnation, conflicts, or corruption stem from weak and fragile institutions [Karl, 1997; Robinson *et al.*, 2006; Sala-i-Martin and Subramanian, 2012; Apergis and Payne, 2014]. Brunnschweiler [2008] argued that institutions play critical roles in the economic growth of natural resource rich countries, and if institutions are functioning soundly, then the natural resource wealth will benefit the economy. Mehlum *et al.* [2006] also argued that resource curse is only seen in resource countries that have bad institutions. The IMF has also emphasized the importance of government capacity and institutional quality in terms of the management of natural resources and revenue [IMF, 2012].

Our interest here is to see whether the development of a financial system favorably influences economic growth in resource countries, as suggested by the existing studies. According to literature on the resource curse, economies depending on natural resource exports, namely "resource-dependent countries," suffer from economic, political, and social problems arising from institutional fragility. In those countries, the development of financial institutions is also likely to be hampered. Financial development may foster growth in resource countries when, for example, foreign direct investment flows into extractive industries, and an increase in resource revenue may create demand for a

122   *Financial Linkages, Remittances, and Resource Dependence in East Asia*

well-functioning financial system. On the other hand, financial development may not favorably affect the economy in resource countries. For example, when resource revenue is exclusively controlled and managed by the government, resource revenue inflow will increase government revenue and disbursement but not necessarily provide investment through private financial intermediation.

Unfortunately, not many analyses of financial development have focused on resource countries. Atkinson and Hamilton [2003] employed the concept of genuine saving and suggest that the savings and investments of resource countries are affected by the quality of institutions and the abundance of natural resources. Sala-i-Martin and Artadi [2002] studied Arab countries on the correlation between investment, growth, and being an oil exporter. They suggested that the slow growth of Arab countries resulted not from lack of investment but rather from low quality of investment, and they pointed out the excessive role of those countries' governments in investment. They concluded that low quality of investment is attributed to the absence of well-functioning financial intermediation and to political and social instability or lack of human capital. Beck [2010] supported this point, demonstrating that the amount of private credit offered by private financial institutions in resource countries is small relative to that in other countries.

Gylfason and Zoega [2006] studied the relationship of economy, saving, investment, and institutions in resource countries and showed that dependence on natural resources is negatively correlated with economic growth. The analysis of Nili and Rastad [2007], based on Sala-i-Martin and Artadi [2002], focused on the quality of investment in oil-exporting countries using GMM with a panel consists of 12 oil-exporting countries and 132 non-oil countries from 1992 to 2001. They showed that while financial institutions are less developed in oil-exporting countries, financial development negatively affects economic growth in those countries. Barajas *et al.* [2013] also showed that financial development and economic growth are negatively correlated, by using cross-term with dummy variables for oil exporters to capture the relationship between financial institutions and growth by relying on macro-panel data.

6.3 Resource Dependence and Abundance

Nili and Rastad [2007], and Barajas *et al.* [2013] analyzed the effects of financial development in resource countries with dynamic panel and using oil-exporter dummy variables or groupings of countries to distinguish oil exporters. In this way, they regarded being a resource exporter as a time invariant, fixed characteristic of a country. However, investments in natural resource development are very active internationally and domestically, and it is not rare to see a country believed to be resource poor become a resource exporter in a few years. Moreover, the amount of production and export, as well as price, fluctuates in the short term, causing the meaning of a natural resource to an economy or society also to vary. If a resource-exporter dummy is created by arbitrary judgment based on the exported amount in a certain year or a period, it will not reflect the real situation of the country.

We therefore prefer not to treat a country as a permanent resource country. Moreover, we distinguish between resource dependence and resource abundance in our model, since they can capture different aspects of a resource country, though resource dependence and resource abundance should be closely correlated. Such distinction of dependence and abundance of natural resource has already been made in an analysis of resource curse conducted by Stijens [2005]. He compared the effects of resource dependence, analyzed by Sachs and Warner [1995], and his own measures of resource abundance on economic growth. His results suggested that resource dependence is indeed negatively correlated with growth rate, but that abundance is not. Gylfason and Zoega [2006] employed the same distinction. On the other hand, Barajas *et al.* [2013] used a variable to measure the economy's dependence on oil but did not distinguish oil abundance.

In our analysis, resource dependence is measured by the share of oil or mining export in a country's economy, as in Barajas *et al.* [2013], with the dependence varying across time. On the other hand, being resource abundant may be a relatively constant characteristic of a country in the short term, compared to resource dependence, if the physical endowment of resources can be accurately measured. However, the natural resource "reserve," which is most likely the only available information on which to build panel data on the resource endowments of countries, is actually increasing as resource exploitation continues and more investment is allocated to exploration and development. Moreover, if resource abundance is measured as per capita resource endowment, it will be affected by population growth in the medium- to long-term. Given the realities of these measures, resource abundance can also be regarded as time-variant.

It should also be noted that both resource dependence and resource abundance can be endogenous to economic growth, though the nature of the correlation seems to be opposite. That is, resource dependence seems to be negatively correlated with growth, since being resource-dependent today may be a reflection of the decline of manufacturing and agriculture due to past failed economic development or a result of conflict, violence, or weak institutions. On the other hand, resource abundance can be, at least theoretically, positively correlated with growth. A large domestic natural resource reserve should reduce spending on imports and provide a good source of revenue. Moreover, if we assume that economic growth and more favorable economic infrastructure will attract more investment in natural resource development, the correlation between economic growth and resource abundance measured by reserve must be positively and simultaneously correlated.

We use the sum of oil and gas (fuel) exports and mining (ores and metal) exports as a share of gross domestic product (GDP) as the variable for evaluating the natural resource dependence of an economy. For resource abundance, we follow Stijens [2005] and use "resource rent" estimated by the World Bank, but calculate per capita resource rent in a real dollar base[a]. Within the system GMM, we use resource dependence and resource abundance as resource weights to make cross terms with financial indicators for assessing the effects of financial development in resource-dependent and resource-abundant countries.

---

[a] We exclude forest rents from our data, such that both resource dependence and resource abundance are measured based on oil, gas, and mining (the metals included in the calculation are described in Appendix 6.2).

Figures 6.1 and 6.2 are scatter plots of those resource weights and per capita GDP in the average of our panel data[b]. They demonstrate that an arbitrary specification of resource countries is not desirable given that in fact not many countries are "non-resource" countries. This also supports our motivation to focus on resource countries.

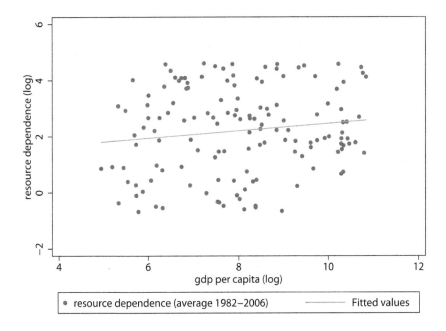

Figure 6.1. Scatter plot of resource dependence.

---

[b] As it can be observed from the difference between the two charts, natural resource export seems to have at least some fractional share in total export even in countries without natural resource. This arises from the definition of the data we used to capture resource dependence, and since we do not have information to adjust re-exports, we used the data as given.

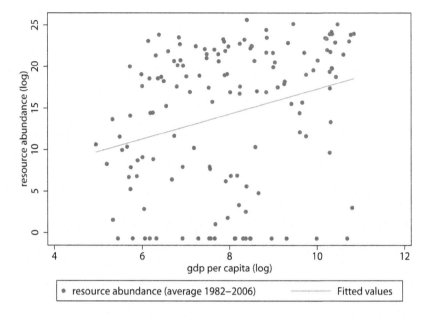

Figure 6.2. Scatter plot of resource abundance.

6.4 Model and Data

Many studies have examined the robustness of the relationship and causality between financial development and growth, particularly in terms of the endogeneity of financial development to growth. Especially for dynamic panel analyses, GMM has become increasingly popular in this area of research. Based on Nili and Rastad [2007], and Barajas *et al.* [2013], we used the system GMM proposed by Arellano and Bond [1991], Arellano and Bover [1995], and Blundell and Bond [1998][c].

---

[c] We used STATA ver.13 for our regression, especially the "xtabond2" command written by David Roodman [Roodman, 2009].

We first consider the equation as follows:

$$y_{i,t} = \alpha y_{i,t-1} + \beta_1 f_{i,t} \times resource + \gamma X_{i,t} + c_i + \mu_t + \varepsilon_{i,t} \quad (6.1)$$

where y is per capita GDP, f is the financial indicator described below, c, μ and ε are the county-specific time invariant effect, period-specific common effect, and error term, respectively. The subscript t denotes a 5-year period, as described below.

To capture the effect of financial development in resource countries, the main interest of this analysis, we include cross terms of financial indicators, with resource dependence and abundance (*resource*) as weights. X is the vector of control variables described below.

As Levine *et al.* [2000] indicates, we can rewrite Eq. (6.1) as

$$y_{i,t} - y_{i,t-1} = (\alpha - 1)y_{i,t-1} + \beta_1 f_{i,t} + \beta_2 f_{i,t} \times resource + \gamma X_{i,t} + c_i + \mu_t + \varepsilon_{i,t}$$

$$(6.2)$$

where the coefficient of the lagged dependent variable captures the convergence effect in economic growth. While some studies employ such a lagged value, we prefer to use initial value ($y_{i,t*in}$), the initial level of GDP per capita of each period (i.e., the first year observation of the respective time period) as in Barajas *et al.* [2013]. We use every variable in natural-log form, and thus the estimated equation can be written as:

$$g_{i,t} = \beta_0 + \beta_1 f_{i,t} + \beta_2 f_{i,t} \times resource + \gamma X_{i,t} + \delta y_{i,t*ini} + c_i + \mu_t + \varepsilon_{i,t}. \quad (6.3)$$

The major motivation for employing GMM in our analysis is to control for unobserved country and time-specific effects and deal with the endogeneity of the explanatory variables in a dynamic regression specification. The system GMM regression combines the level and difference equations using the lagged explanatory variables as instruments. Given the size of our panel, we include the second to fourth lags of levels as instruments for difference estimators to limit the proliferation of instruments, and this setting results in inclusion of only one-term lags of differences as instruments for the level estimators

[Roodman, 2009]. We include period dummies in every regression to control for the time-specific effect μ.

Levine *et al.* [2000] used GMM for a panel of 74 countries, while Barajas *et al.* [2013] expanded the coverage of countries to 150 countries in maximum by incorporating IMF internal data. Both of them constructed a small T, large N panel, suitable for the application of system GMM, by taking nonoverlapping 5-year averages of data. We have followed their method and tried to cover as many countries as possible, especially relatively less developed countries, because many of the current resource-dependent countries are developing countries. We have included 140 countries in our panel, between 1982 and 2006, though not strictly balanced. We take the average of the data for each

Table 6.1.   Descriptive statistics and correlations.

	g	*ini*	*m2*	*cred*	*edu*	*fdi*	*open*	*infl*	*dpd*	*abd*
Obs.	542	664	645	617	646	670	685	634	582	686
Mean	0.08	1.59	3.71	3.20	3.97	4.09	4.17	3.34	2.23	14.24
S.D.	0.13	0.32	0.63	0.95	0.76	0.05	0.53	0.54	1.54	9.02
Min.	-0.54	0.95	1.92	0.09	1.32	3.99	2.42	2.64	-0.69	-0.69
Max.	0.46	2.23	5.42	5.22	5.05	4.34	5.46	7.22	4.61	26.16

Correlation (Pairwise)

	g	*ini*	*m2*	*cred*	*edu*	*fdi*	*open*	*infl*	*dpd*	*abd*
g	1									
ini	0.15	1								
m2	0.26	0.59	1							
cred	0.28	0.71	0.81	1						
edu	0.21	0.77	0.60	0.63	1					
fdi	0.32	0.11	0.25	0.16	0.17	1				
open	0.18	0.21	0.31	0.25	0.26	0.46	1			
infl	-0.35	-0.17	-0.29	-0.38	-0.09	-0.14	-0.23	1		
dpd	-0.26	0.09	-0.15	-0.13	0.04	-0.19	-0.09	0.13	1	
abd	-0.06	0.25	0.06	0.13	0.23	-0.14	-0.21	0.11	0.57	1

Notes: Calculated from data in natural-log. Abbreviations are used for g (per capita growth); *ini* (initial gdp per capita); *cred* (private credit); *edu* (education); *open* (openness); *infl* (inflation); *dpd* (dependence); *abd* (abundance).

period of nonoverlapping five years, resulting in five periods: 1982–1986, 1987–1991, 1992–1996, 1997–2001, and 2002–2006. To deal with heterogeneity in the data, we used two-step system GMM. The countries included in the sample are shown in Appendix 6.1.

The degree of financial development of each country is measured by several variables in existing literature. As the countries of our focus are often less developed and thus not equipped with highly developed financial services, we use the most widely available data—the ratio of liquidity in liabilities (M2) to GDP and the ratio of private credit by deposit money banks (private credit) to GDP—to maximize the coverage of countries. We obtained the data on M2 from the World Development Indicators of the World Bank [2014]. The data on private credit was obtained from the Financial Development and Structure Dataset [Beck *et al.*, 2000; 2009; Čihák *et al.*, 2012].

We have included several control variables that also have been employed in similar studies, such as human capital (measured by the gross secondary-education enrollment ratio), net foreign direct investment inflow as a ratio of GDP, openness of trade measured by the ratio of trade to GDP, and the annual inflation rate measured by the changes in the consumer price index. Those data are also obtained from World Development Indicators. Summary statistics are reported in Table 6.1, and detailed definitions of variables and data source are listed in Appendix 6.2.

6.5 Results

Regarding the sample size and robustness of system GMM estimation, Windmeijer [2005] and Roodman [2009] pointed out that standard errors can be underestimated with small sample and they suggest corrections for the problem. In Windmeijer [2005], a $T=4$, $N=100$ panel is discussed as a small panel. Although our sample size is slightly larger, consisting of $T=5$ and $N=140$ at maximum, not a few observations lack in our data depending on the model and the inclusion of control variables. Therefore, we have adopted corrections and reported standard errors are clustered by country based on Roodman [2009]. We also report the results of specification tests on the validity of instruments: the Hansen test for overidentifying restriction and the test for serial correlation [Arellano and Bond, 1991; Roodman, 2009].

Tables 6.2 and 6.3 show the regression results of dynamic panel analysis using system GMM. When liquidity in liabilities, M2, is used as the financial indicator (Table 6.2), the coefficient of M2 enters with a positive sign, though it is not statistically significant in most regressions. The coefficient of the cross term with resource dependence consistently enters with a negative sign with statistical significance. On the other hand, the coefficient of the cross term with resource abundance has neither stable sign nor significance. On the other hand, when private credit is used as the financial indicator (Table 6.3), the coefficient of private credit is positive and statistically significant in some regressions, though the sign turns negative and not significant when inflation is controlled. Similar to the regressions using M2, the cross term with resource dependence enters with a negative sign and is statistically significant in most of the regressions. Here the cross term with resource abundance has a positive sign and is stable though not always statistically significant. In all regressions, Hansen test statistics are large enough and the second-order serial correlations are weak enough that the set of instruments can be regarded as valid.

These results, in general, suggest a strong and consistent negative correlation between financial development and economic growth in resource-dependent countries. In other words, the growth-promoting effect of financial development is weaker in resource-dependent countries than in other countries. On the other hand, financial development is not necessarily negatively correlated with growth in resource-abundant countries, or is weakly but positively correlated when we measure financial development by private credit.

Table 6.2. Financial development and growth: Dynamic panel, system GMM
[M2 as financial indicator].

	Dependent variable: growth per capita					
	(1)	(2)	(3)	(4)	(5)	(6)
M2	0.0496	0.0741	0.0472	0.0462	0.0472	0.0649*
	[0.050]	[0.057]	[0.043]	[0.051]	[0.043]	[0.035]
M2× resource dependence	-0.0120***		-0.0112**	-0.0081	-0.0112**	-0.0133***
	[0.004]		[0.005]	[0.007]	[0.005]	[0.004]
M2× resource abundance		-0.0016	-0.0004	0.000	-0.0004	0.0006
		[0.001]	[0.001]	[0.001]	[0.001]	[0.001]
Initial GDP per capita	0.0166	-0.0917	0.0088	-0.0145	0.0088	-0.2048
	[0.137]	[0.138]	[0.133]	[0.145]	[0.133]	[0.129]
Education	0.0214	0.0796	0.027	0.0239	0.027	0.0343
	[0.069]	[0.056]	[0.058]	[0.072]	[0.058]	[0.057]
FDI				0.5272		
				[0.531]		
Trade openness						0.0667
						[0.076]
Inflation						
period2	-0.0296		-0.024	-0.0054	-0.024	-0.0017
	[0.022]		[0.022]	[0.026]	[0.022]	[0.029]
period3	-0.0375	-0.0061	-0.0388	-0.0382	-0.0388	-0.0440*
	[0.024]	[0.019]	[0.024]	[0.026]	[0.024]	[0.023]
period4	0.0089	0.0306	0.0053	0.01	0.0053	0.0099
	[0.011]	[0.022]	[0.010]	[0.012]	[0.010]	[0.011]
period5		0.0241				
		[0.025]				
Constant	-0.1177	-0.2973***	-0.099	-2.2531	-0.099	-0.1644
	[0.144]	[0.094]	[0.144]	[2.134]	[0.144]	[0.289]
n	412	469	412	410	412	410
n of Countries	134	140	134	134	134	134
n of Instruments	41	41	50	59	50	59
Hansen statistics	0.063	0.063	0.179	0.108	0.179	0.074
AR2 test (p-value)	0.847	0.316	0.863	0.426	0.863	0.172

(*Continued*)

Table 6.2. (*Continued*)

	(7)	(8)	(9)	(10)	(11)
	Dependent variable: growth per capita				
M2	0.0345	0.0608	0.0074	0.0331	0.0167
	[0.047]	[0.039]	[0.052]	[0.043]	[0.039]
M2× resource	-0.0165***	-0.0123***	-0.0093*		-0.0080*
dependence	[0.005]	[0.005]	[0.005]		[0.004]
M2× resource	0.001	0.0011		0.0012	0.0003
abundance	[0.001]	[0.001]		[0.001]	[0.001]
Initial GDP per	-0.1437	-0.1373	-0.3576***	-0.2275*	-0.2809**
capita	[0.120]	[0.101]	[0.133]	[0.117]	[0.113]
Education	0.0119	0.0269	0.1699***	0.0710*	0.1373***
	[0.057]	[0.055]	[0.058]	[0.038]	[0.048]
FDI	1.5421**	0.4758	0.3878	0.9884**	0.4569
	[0.747]	[0.503]	[0.440]	[0.384]	[0.415]
Trade openness		-0.0183	-0.0038	0.0161	0.0064
		[0.074]	[0.071]	[0.057]	[0.063]
Inflation			-0.1788***	-0.1466***	-0.1589***
			[0.052]	[0.035]	[0.044]
period2	0.0251				
	[0.025]				
period3	-0.0064	-0.0328*	-0.0489**	-0.0186	-0.0499**
	[0.021]	[0.019]	[0.022]	[0.019]	[0.022]
period4	0.014	0.0156	-0.0348	-0.0322	-0.036
	[0.013]	[0.023]	[0.023]	[0.021]	[0.022]
period5		0.0011	-0.0428*	-0.0536**	-0.0472*
		[0.023]	[0.026]	[0.023]	[0.025]
Constant	-6.1123**	-1.8627	-0.9346	-3.6345***	-1.3735
	[3.002]	[1.936]	[1.736]	[1.370]	[1.667]
n	410	408	387	436	387
n of Countries	134	134	128	134	128
n of Instruments	59	68	68	68	77
Hansen statistics	0.270	0.165	0.123	0.126	0.172
AR2 test (p-value)	0.324	0.282	0.552	0.476	0.500

Notes: Robust standard errors in parentheses. Stars are attached to denote * $p<0.05$, ** $p<0.01$, *** $p<0.001$. Period dummies are from 1 to 5 for 1982–1986, 1987–1991, 1992–1996, 1997–2001, and 2002–2006, respectively. The null hypothesis of AR2 test is no second-order serial correlation in the difference regression.

Table 6.3. Financial development and growth: Dynamic panel, system GMM [Private credit as financial indicator].

	(1)	(2)	(3)	(4)	(5)	(6)
	Dependent variable: growth per capita					
Private credit	0.0725*	0.0734**	0.0733*	0.0491	0.0733*	0.0736**
	[0.038]	[0.031]	[0.041]	[0.035]	[0.041]	[0.036]
Prv. credit× resource dependence	-0.0083		-0.0097*	-0.0084	-0.0097*	-0.0149***
	[0.005]		[0.006]	[0.006]	[0.006]	[0.004]
Prv. credit× resource abundance		0.0002	0.0004	0.0006	0.0004	0.0009
		[0.001]	[0.001]	[0.001]	[0.001]	[0.001]
Initial GDP per capita	-0.1371	-0.0978	-0.1367	-0.0933	-0.1367	-0.2528*
	[0.135]	[0.114]	[0.112]	[0.117]	[0.112]	[0.146]
Education	0.0404	0.0166	0.0304	0.0458	0.0304	0.0453
	[0.049]	[0.041]	[0.041]	[0.053]	[0.041]	[0.041]
FDI				0.3125		
				[0.471]		
Trade openness						0.023
						[0.059]
Inflation						
period2	-0.0172		-0.0049		-0.0049	-0.0016
	[0.022]		[0.021]		[0.021]	[0.024]
period3	-0.0366**	0.0054	-0.0214	-0.0232	-0.0214	-0.0279
	[0.019]	[0.015]	[0.018]	[0.016]	[0.018]	[0.019]
period4	0.0164	0.0477***	0.0167	0.0138	0.0167	0.0147
	[0.013]	[0.017]	[0.010]	[0.021]	[0.010]	[0.011]
period5		0.031		-0.0058		
		[0.022]		[0.023]		
Constant	-0.0421	-0.1049	-0.0193	-1.362	-0.0193	0.0316
	[0.135]	[0.099]	[0.135]	[1.841]	[0.135]	[0.219]
n	404	453	404	401	404	404
n of Countries	130	136	130	130	130	130
n of Instruments	50	50	50	59	50	59
Hansen	0.273	0.306	0.625	0.485	0.625	0.378
AR2	0.365	0.565	0.441	0.683	0.441	0.923

(*Continued*)

Table 6.3. (*Continued*)

	Dependent variable: growth per capita				
	(7)	(8)	(9)	(10)	(11)
Private credit	0.0325	0.0496	0.0248	0.0004	-0.0124
	[0.033]	[0.035]	[0.032]	[0.027]	[0.033]
Private credit × resource dependence	-0.0093*	-0.0147***	-0.0136***		-0.0135***
	[0.005]	[0.005]	[0.005]		[0.005]
Private credit × resource abundance	0.0007	0.0011**		0.0012**	0.001
	[0.001]	[0.000]		[0.001]	[0.001]
Initial GDP per capita	-0.0869	-0.1812	-0.3719***	-0.2081**	-0.2379***
	[0.118]	[0.114]	[0.126]	[0.099]	[0.092]
Education	0.0433	0.0514	0.1808***	0.0743**	0.1398***
	[0.058]	[0.044]	[0.049]	[0.037]	[0.037]
FDI	0.5647	0.2464	0.2411	1.0061**	0.5103
	[0.402]	[0.457]	[0.330]	[0.402]	[0.336]
Trade openness		0.0208	0.0054	0.0017	-0.0247
		[0.057]	[0.051]	[0.042]	[0.041]
Inflation			-0.1877***	-0.1459***	-0.1878***
			[0.050]	[0.038]	[0.043]
period2				0.0479**	
				[0.021]	
period3	-0.0302**	-0.0262*	-0.0474**	0.033	-0.0454**
	[0.015]	[0.016]	[0.020]	[0.021]	[0.019]
period4	0.007	0.0114	-0.0449**	0.0165	-0.0428**
	[0.020]	[0.023]	[0.021]	[0.011]	[0.019]
period5	-0.0083	-0.0079	-0.0495**		-0.0429**
	[0.022]	[0.024]	[0.021]		[0.021]
Constant	-2.3362	-1.0413	-0.4011	-3.6104**	-1.3517
	[1.553]	[1.789]	[1.365]	[1.557]	[1.425]
n	401	401	393	440	393
n of Countries	130	130	128	134	128
n of Instruments	68	68	68	68	77
Hansen	0.519	0.477	0.252	0.171	0.230
AR2	0.954	0.875	0.831	0.539	0.569

Notes: Robust standard errors in parentheses. Stars are attached to denote * $p<0.05$, ** $p<0.01$, *** $p<0.001$. Period dummies are from 1 to 5 for 1982–1986, 1987–1991, 1992–1996, 1997–2001, and 2002–2006, respectively. The null hypothesis of AR2 test is no second-order serial correlation in the difference regression.

6.6 Role of Institutions

Given the results of the dynamic panel analysis, we should now consider why the growth-promoting effect of financial development is weaker in resource-dependent countries than in other countries. Several reasons can be raised regarding obstacles to fostering economic growth in resource countries, as briefly discussed above in terms of the resource curse. On the other hand, the bottleneck for smooth transmission of a growth-promoting effect of financial functioning is less clear. Sala-i-Martin and Artadi [2002] suggest that in Arab oil countries the absence of political and social instability is the possible reason to disturb financial mechanisms. Based on the literature, we also consider that the quality of institutions seems to play a part in determining the sound functioning of financial mechanisms and economic activities.

To test our hypothesis that low quality of institutions is a disturbance factor in transmission of the growth-promoting effect of financial development, we attempted to explicitly control for institutional quality by use of a variable in our dynamic panel analysis. The literature analyzing the effect of institutions, including Brunnschweiler [2008], uses The World Governance Indicators (WGI) according to Kaufman *et al.* [2005]. However, the data in WGI is available only since 1996, even though they are updated [Kaufman *et al.*, 2010]. The other possible information source for data on institutional quality is limited in country coverage. This data limitation prevents us from maintaining our sample size and including the governance indicators into our dynamic panel analysis.

We instead have resorted to a brief, static review of the relationship between institutional quality and financial development. We calculate correlation coefficients of governance indicators available from WGI as proxies for institutional quality, financial indicators used in the panel, and resource dependence and resource abundance used as weights in the panel. As shown in Table 6.4, the pairwise correlation coefficients between financial indicators and governance indicators are positive, large, and statistically significant. On the other hand, the resource weights, especially resource dependence, are negatively correlated with all of the government indicators, though the coefficients are not large and

Table 6.4. Correlations of institutional quality, financial development and natural resources.

	M2	Private credit	Resource dependence	Resource abundance
Control of corruption	0.65*	0.76*	-0.08	0.06
Government effectiveness	0.69*	0.79*	-0.06	0.12
Political stability and absence of violence / terrorism	0.50*	0.57*	-0.17*	-0.14
Regulatory quality	0.63*	0.74*	-0.08	0.07
Rule of law	0.70*	0.78*	-0.16*	-0.00
Voice and accountability	0.59*	0.69*	-0.31*	-0.12

Notes: Pairwise correlation coefficients. * denotes p-value < 0.05. Calculated from the average data between 1996 and 2006. M2, private credit, resource dependence, and resource abundance are the same data as used in the panel analysis. The indicators of institutional quality are taken from WGI. For detailed definition of indicators, see Kaufman *et al.* [2005] and Kaufman *et al.* [2010]. Governance indicators are the average of the data for year 1996, 1998, 2000, and 2002 to 2006.

not always statistically significant. This implies that while financial development and institutional quality improvement very often occur in parallel, natural resource dependence tends to be associated with lower institutional quality as measured by various indicators.

6.7 Conclusions

The results of our dynamic panel analysis strongly suggest that the linkage between financial development and growth is weaker in countries that depend on natural resource exports. This conclusion is consistent with similar studies such as Nili and Rastad [2007], and Barajas *et al.* [2013]. On the other hand, in resource-abundant countries, financial development is likely to be correlated with positive growth, or at least there is no factor to weaken the effect of financial development on growth.

The results are consistent with the resource curse scenario, in terms of a correlation between low institutional quality and low financial development, though this argument still must be supported by dynamic analysis.

The problems categorized as resource curse are often believed to be suffered by a small number of oil-exporting countries. However, as we have shown, there are not many purely "non-resource" countries, and our analysis of data on both oil exporters and other resource countries suggests the possibility that the problems associated with resource dependence can be, in fact, more generally seen in non-oil-exporter countries. We have also distinguished the various aspects of resource countries, and have clarified the difference between resource dependence and resource abundance with respect to financial development and growth.

There are many points still left to be analyzed. In particular, the extension of the sample period to include the recent global financial crisis is required to derive a more general understanding of the relationship between financial development and the economy in resource countries.

Appendix 6.1 List of countries included in the sample

OECD	High income: nonOECD	Upper middle income	
Australia	Bahamas, The	Albania	St. Lucia
Austria	Bahrain	Algeria	St. Vincent and
Belgium	Barbados	Angola	the Grenadines
Canada	Brunei Darussalam	Argentina	Thailand
Chile	Croatia	Belize	Tonga
Czech Republic	Cyprus	Botswana	Tunisia
Denmark	Kuwait	Brazil	Turkey
Estonia	Latvia	Bulgaria	Venezuela
Finland	Lithuania	Colombia	
France	Malta	Costa Rica	
Germany	Oman	Dominica	
Greece	Qatar	Dominican Republic	
Iceland	Russian Federation	Ecuador	
Ireland	Saudi Arabia	Fiji	
Israel	St. Kitts and Nevis	Gabon	
Italy	Trinidad and Tobago	Grenada	
Japan	United Arab Emirates	Hungary	
Korea, Rep.	Uruguay	Iran	
Netherlands		Jordan	
New Zealand		Kazakhstan	
Norway		Lebanon	
Poland		Libya	
Portugal		Malaysia	
Slovak Republic		Mauritius	
Slovenia		Mexico	
Spain		Namibia	
Sweden		Panama	
Switzerland		Peru	
United Kingdom		Romania	
United States		Serbia	
		South Africa	

List of countries included in the sample (continued)

Lower middle income		Low income
Bolivia	Ukraine	Bangladesh
Cabo Verde	Uzbekistan	Benin
Cameroon	Vanuatu	Burkina Faso
Congo, Rep.	Vietnam	Burundi
Cote d'Ivoire	Yemen	Cambodia
Egypt	Zambia	Central African Republic
El Salvador		Chad
Ghana		Ethiopia
Guatemala		Gambia, The
Guyana		Haiti
Honduras		Kenya
India		Madagascar
Indonesia		Malawi
Lao PDR		Mali
Lesotho		Mozambique
Mauritania		Nepal
Mongolia		Niger
Morocco		Rwanda
Nigeria		Tanzania
Pakistan		Togo
Papua New Guinea		Uganda
Paraguay		Zimbabwe
Philippines		
Samoa		
Senegal		
Solomon Islands		
Sri Lanka		
Sudan		
Swaziland		
Syrian Arab Republic		

Notes: Income categories are according to the World Bank.

Appendix 6.2 Data sources and definitions of variables used in panel

Variable	Definition	Source
GDP per capita	Real GDP per capita (constant 2005 US$)	WDI
M2	Money and quasi money as % of GDP	WDI
Private credit	Private credit by deposit money banks to GDP (%)	FDSD
Resource dependence	Ores and metals exports + Fuel exports	
Ores and metals exports	Share of merchandize export of Ores and metals; SITC sections 27 (crude fertilizer, minerals nes); 28 (metalliferous ores, scrap); and 68 (non-ferrous metals).	WDI
Fuel exports	Share of merchandize export of Fuels; SITC section 3 (mineral fuels).	WDI
Resource abundance	Resource rent (oil+coal+gas+mineral)*real GDP/population	
Oil rents (% of GDP)	The difference between the value of crude oil production at world prices and total costs of production.	WDI
Coal rents	The difference between the value of both hard and soft coal production at world prices and their total costs of production.	WDI
Gas rents	The difference between the value of natural gas production at world prices and total costs of production.	WDI
Mineral rents	The difference between the value of production for a stock of minerals at world prices and their total costs of production. Minerals included are tin, gold, lead, zinc, iron, copper, nickel, silver, bauxite, and phosphate.	WDI
GDP	Real GDP (constant 2005 US$)	WDI
Population	Total population.	WDI
Education	Gross secondary education enrollment ratio (%)	WDI
FDI	Foreign direct investment, net inflows as % of GDP	WDI
Trade openness	Exports + imports of goods and services, as % of GDP	WDI
Inflation	Measured by the consumer price index, annual percentage change (%)	WDI

References

Apergis, N. and Payne, J. E. (2014). The oil curse, institutional quality, and growth in MENA countries: Evidence from time-varying cointegration, *Energy Economics*, 46, pp. 1–9.

Arellano, M. and Bond, S. (1991). Some tests of specification for panel data: Monte Carlo evidence and application to employment equations, *The Review of Economic Studies*, 58(2), pp. 277–297.

Arellano, M. and Bover, O. (1995). Another look at the instrumental variable estimation of error-components models, *Journal of Econometrics*, 68, pp. 29–51.

Atkinson, G. and Hamilton, K. (2003). Savings, growth and the resource curse hypothesis, *World Development*, 31, pp. 1793–1807.

Barajas, A., Chami, R. and Yousefi, S. R. (2013). The finance and growth nexus re-examined: Do all countries benefit equally? *IMF Working Paper* WP/13/130.

Beck, T. (2010). Finance and oil: Is there a resource curse in financial development? *European Banking Center Discussion Paper* No. 2011-004.

Beck, T., Demirgüç-Kunt, A. and Levine, R. (2000). A New Database on Financial Development and Structure, *World Bank Economic Review*, 14, pp. 597–605.

Beck, T., Demirgüç-Kunt, A. and Levine, R. (2009). Financial Institutions and Markets across Countries and over Time: Data and Analysis, *Policy Research Working Paper Series* 4943, The World Bank.

Brunnschweiler, C. N. (2008). Cursing the blessings? Natural resource abundance, institutions, and economic growth, *World Development*, 36(3), pp. 399–419.

Blundell, R. and Bond, S. (1998). Initial conditions and moment restrictions in dynamic panel data models, *Journal of Econometrics*, 87, pp. 115–143.

Čihák, M., Demirgüç-Kunt, A., Feyen, E. and Levine, R. (2012). Benchmarking Financial Development around the World. *Policy Research Working Paper Series* 6175, The World Bank.

Collier, P. and Hoeffler, A. (2004). Greed and grievance in civil war, *Oxford Economic Paper*, 56, pp. 563–595.

Corden, M. W. (1981). The exchange rate, monetary policy and North Sea oil: The economic theory of the squeeze of tradable, *Oxford Economic Papers*, New Series 31, Supplement, pp. 23–46.

Corden, M. W. (1984). Booming Sector and Dutch Disease Economics: Survey and Consolidation, *Oxford Economic Papers*, New Series 36(3), pp. 359–380.

Corden, M. W. and Neary, J. P. (1982). Booming Sector and De-Industrialisation in a Small Open Economy, *The Economic Journal*, 92, pp. 825–848.

Demigüç-Kunt, A. and Levine, R. (2008). Finance, financial sector policies, and long-run growth, *Policy Research Working Paper* 4469, The World Bank.

Gylfason, T. and Zoega, G. (2006). Natural Resources and Economic Growth: The Role of investment, *The World Economy*, 29(8), pp. 1091–1115.

IMF (2012). Macroeconomic Policy Frameworks for Resource-Rich Developing Countries, International Monetary Fund. Available at http://www.imf.org/external/np/pp/eng/2012/082412.pdf (last accessed on May 19, 2014).

Karl, T. L. (1997). *Paradox of Plenty* (University of California Press, Berkeley and Los Angeles).

Kaufmann, D., Kraay, A. and Mastruzzi, M. (2005). Governance matters IV: Governance indicators for 1996−2004, *Policy Research Working Paper Series* 3630, The World Bank.

Kaufmann, D., Kraay, A. and Mastruzzi, M. (2010). The Worldwide Governance Indicators: A Summary of Methodology, Data and Analytical Issues, *World Bank Policy Research Working Paper Series* 5430, The World Bank.

King, R. G. and Levine, R. (1993). Finance and growth; Schumpeter might be right, *The Quarterly Journal of Economics*, 108 (3), pp. 717–737.

Levine, R. (1997). Financial development and economic growth: Views and agenda, *Journal of Economic Literature*, 35 (2), pp. 688–726.

Levine, R., Loayza, N. and Beck, T. (2000). Financial intermediation and growth: Causality and causes, *Journal of Monetary Economics*, 46, pp. 31–77.

Levine, R. and Renelt, D. (1992). A sensitivity analysis of cross-country growth regressions, *The American Economic Review*, 82(4), pp. 942–963.

Mehlum, H., Moene, K., and Torvik, R. (2006). Institutions and the resource curse, *The Economic Journal*, 116, pp. 1–20.

Nili, M. and Rastad, M. (2007). Addressing the growth failure of the oil economies: The role of financial development, *The Quarterly Review of Economics and Finance*, 46, pp. 726–740.

Robinson, J.A., Torbvik, R., and Vedier, T. (2006). Political foundations of the resource curse, *Journal of Development Economics*, 79, pp. 447–468.

Roodman, D. (2009). How to do xtabond2: An introduction to difference and system GMM in Stata, *The Stata Journal*, 9(1), pp. 86–136.

Sala-i-Martin, X. and Artadi, E. V. (2002). Economic Growth and Investment in the Arab World, *Department of Economics Discussion Paper Series* 0203-08 (Columbia University).

Sala-i-Martin, X. and Subramanian A. (2012). Addressing the Natural Resource Curse: An illustration from Nigeria, *Journal of African Economies*, 22(4), pp. 570–615.

Sachs, J. D. and Warner, A. M. (1995). Natural resource abundance and economic growth, *NBER Working Paper* 5398.

Sachs, J. D. and Warner, A. M. (2001). Natural resources and economic development: The curse of natural Resources, *European Economic Review*, 45, pp. 827–838.

Stijens, J. (2005). Natural resource abundance and economic growth revisited, *Resource Policy*, 30, pp. 107–130.

Windmeijer, F. (2005). A finite sample correction for the variance of linear efficient two-step GMM estimators, *Journal of Econometrics*, 126, pp. 25–51.

World Bank (2014). *World Development Indicators 2014.* Washington, DC: World Bank. Available at http://databank.worldbank.org/data/ (Accessed on 7 Nov, 2014).
Yusof, Z. A. (2011). The Developmental State: Malaysia, in Collier, P. and Venables, A. J. Eds., Plundered Nations? Successes and Failures in natural Resource Extraction (Palgrave Macmillan, Hampshire and New York) pp. 188–230.

Part III

Policy Priorities for the Financial Integration and Management of Resource-Rich Economies

Chapter 7

Spillovers of Financial Stress Shocks: Evidence and Policy Implications

Wang Chen

Graduate School of Economics, Kobe University

2-1, Rokkodai, Nada-Ku, Kobe 657-8501, Japan

Email: tinou3776@yahoo.co.jp

Takuji Kinkyo

Faculty of Economics, Kobe University

2-1, Rokkodai, Nada-Ku, Kobe 657-8501, Japan

Email: kinkyo@econ.kobe-u.ac.jp

7.1   Introduction

Since the global financial crisis of 2007–2009, there has been a renewed interest in cross-border spillovers of financial stress shocks among policy makers. Financial stress is a disruption to the functioning of financial markets, which adversely affects real economic activity. The origin of the global financial crisis was the US subprime mortgage debacle triggered by the bursting of the housing market bubble. This housing loan crisis developed into a systemic financial crisis after the collapse of so-called shadow-banking systems. The deepening of the crisis caused serious disruptions in the US financial markets. In the wake of the collapse of Lehman Brothers in September 2008, the US financial stress spread rapidly to the rest of the world. Asian economies were also hit hard by sudden capital withdrawals, triggering a sharp fall in stock prices [IMF, 2009]. In response, internationally coordinated efforts have been made to increase the resilience of global financial systems by promoting various regulatory reforms. However, the question remains as to whether these global financial systems will then become significantly more resilient.

Against this background, this chapter aims to contribute to the literature by analyzing the cross-border spillover effects of US financial stress shocks on Asian stock markets. Following Eichenbaum and Evans' [1995] seminal work, many studies have identified monetary policy shocks and examined their cross-border spillover effects [Artis *et al.*, 2007; Canova, 2005; Holman and Neuman, 2002; Kim, 2001; Mackowiak, 2007; Neri and Nobili, 2010]. By comparison, significantly fewer analyses have been conducted to identify financial stress shocks and examine their cross-border spillover effects. However, the global financial crisis has stimulated empirical research on financial stress shocks. Some important contributions include Fornari and Stracca [2012], Galesi and Sgherri [2009], and Helbling *et al.* [2011].

The remainder of the paper is organized as follows. Section 2 reviews the literature on cross-border spillovers of financial stress shocks. Section 3 describes the econometric method. Section 4 presents estimation results. Section 5 discusses the policy implications. Section 6 concludes.

7.2   Cross-border Spillovers of Financial Stress Shocks

The financial stress can depress business and household spending through greater volatility in asset prices, higher funding costs, and the reduced availability of bank credit. Empirical evidence indicates that financial stress is associated with significant and long-lasting negative effects on economic activity [Cerra and Saxena, 2008; Reinhart and Rogoff, 2009]. In addition, financial stress in one country can be transmitted to other countries through a variety of channels.[a] One possible channel for the spillovers of financial stress is trade linkages. Financial stress can depress domestic spending and thus the associated demand for imports, reducing exports from trading partners. Moreover, if the central bank responds to financial stress by easing monetary policy, the exchange rate will depreciate, exerting a beggar-thy-neighbour effect on export competitors. Eichengreen *et al.,* [1996] find evidence for the spillover of shocks through trade linkages.

Another important channel for financial spillovers is financial linkages. Empirical evidence indicates that financial shocks spread mostly through financial linkages [IMF, 2013]. Financial stress can force banks to curtail lending not only within national borders but also across borders, reducing liquidity and raising the cost of credit in the affected foreign countries. Kaminsky and Reinhart [2000] show that the presence of common financial linkages through bank lending can better explain the pattern of financial spillovers across countries. Likewise, financial stress can force portfolio investors to sell assets in foreign countries to meet margin calls and rebalance portfolio according to time-varying risk profiles. Based on an extensive literature survey, Gelos [2011] concludes that the portfolio rebalancing mechanism is important in explaining financial spillover patterns across countries. Raddatz and Schmukler [2012] use micro-level data on mutual funds and show that the procyclical nature of mutual fund investment tends to have destabilising spillover effects.

Finally, a variant of financial spillovers through financial linkages is a "wake-up call" channel. Goldstein [1998] originally used this term to describe the sudden reappraisal of risks in the Asian financial systems, which induced capital flow reversals during the financial crisis of 1997–98. More broadly, a reappraisal of risks in one country can serve as a wake-up call to urge investors to reassess the risk in other countries that share the similar vulnerabilities. As a result of risk reassessment,

---

[a] Forbes [2012] provides an excellent survey of literature on cross-border spillovers of economic shocks, which is often referred to as contagion.

investors will call in loans and sell assets across countries, thereby causing financial spillovers. Forbes [2012] measures the wake-up channel by using dummy variables for credit ratings and shows that the spillover effect through this channel is statistically significant.

To summarise, the existing literature indicates that financial stress in one country can be transmitted to foreign countries through various channels, exerting cross-border spillover effects on their financial markets, including stock markets.

7.3   Econometric Method

In this section, we follow Kilian's [2009] method to identify financial stress shocks and estimate their impacts on Asian stock prices. Kilian [2009] uses a two-step procedure to analyze the macroeconomic effects of oil price shocks. In the first step, a vector autoregression (VAR) model is estimated to identify three types of structural shocks, oil supply, aggregate demand, and oil market-specific demand shocks, which reflect an unexpected change in precautionary oil demand. In the second step, ordinary least squares (OLS) regressions are estimated to evaluate the effects of the identified structural shocks on macroeconomic variables. Kilian [2009] adopts this framework to demonstrate that US macroeconomic variables respond differently to oil price shocks depending on the underlying shock types. Recent studies have employed and extended this framework to examine how oil price shocks affect real economic activity and financial markets in the United States and elsewhere [Apergis and Miller, 2009; Kilian and Park, 2009; Yoshizaki and Hamori, 2013; Chen *et al.*, 2014].

We first identify US structural shocks by estimating a VAR model, which includes a real activity shock, a financial stress shock, and a monetary policy shock. The model's structural representation is

$$A_0 y_t = \alpha + \sum_{i=1}^{p} A_i y_{t-i} + \varepsilon_t \qquad (7.1)$$

where y_t is a (3×1) vector containing variables for real economic activity, financial market conditions, and monetary policy stances. A_0 denotes a contemporaneous coefficient matrix, α denotes a vector of constant terms, and ε_t denotes a vector of serially and mutually uncorrelated structural shocks. Under the appropriate identifying restrictions, structural shocks can be recovered from the estimated reduced-form errors using the following relationship:

$$e_t = A_0^{-1} \varepsilon_t \qquad (7.2)$$

where e_t denotes the reduced-form errors.

US real economic activity is measured by the Chicago Fed National Activity Index (CFNAI), a weighted average of the 85 economic indicators of US economic activity[b]. A positive value indicates that US economic growth is above the trend, whereas a negative value indicates the opposite. US financial market conditions are measured by the Kansas City Financial Stress Index (KCFSI), which is a comprehensive, composite index designed to measure the stress level in US financial markets[c]. Monetary policy stances are measured by the Federal funds (FF) rate.

The VAR is estimated using the levels of the CFNAI and the KCFSI and the first difference of the FF rate[d]. The sample period is from

---

[b] The economic indicators are derived from four broad categories: (1) production and income; (2) employment, unemployment, and hours; (3) personal consumption and housing; (4) sales, orders, and inventories. Further details of the index and data can be obtained at http://www.chicagofed.org/webpages/publications/cfnai/.

[c] The KCFSI was developed by the Federal Reserve Bank of Kansas City, It is a principal-component measure of the following 11 financial variables: 3-month TED spread, 2-year swap spread, off-the-run/on-the-run 10-year Treasury spread, Aaa/10-year Treasury spread, Baa/Aaa spread, high-yield bond/Baa spread, consumer ABS/5-year Treasury spread, the correlation between stock and Treasury returns, the implied volatility of overall stock prices, the idiosyncratic volatility of bank stock prices, and the cross-sectional dispersion of bank stock returns. Hakkio and Keeton [2009] discuss its key features in detail.

[d] The first difference of the FF rate is used, because the level of the variable is non-stationary according to the augmented Dickey–Fuller test. All transformed variables are stationary at the 5% significance level.

January 1990 to December 2012. The lag length is set to 9 months according to the Akaike Information Criterion (AIC).

We identify structural shocks using the Choleski decomposition, with the order being the CFNAI, the KCFSI, and the FF rate. This order determines the exogeneity of the variables: a shock to a particular variable has a contemporaneous effect on the variables ordered after that particular variable but not before it. Following Bernanke *et al.*, [2005], the FF rate is ordered last, implying that the Fed monitors a wide range of information and sets an FF rate target in response to contemporaneous changes in real economic activity and financial market conditions. The CFNAI is before the KCFSI because the real activity shock is assumed to have contemporaneous effects on financial markets but not vice versa. By adopting this order, we assume that real activity, financial stress, and monetary policy shocks can be captured by a structural shock to the CFNAI, the KCFSI, and the FF rate, respectively. Hence, the reduced-form VAR is obtained by multiplying both sides of Eq. (7.1) by A_0^{-1}, which has the following recursive structure:

$$\begin{pmatrix} u_{1t} \\ u_{2t} \\ u_{3t} \end{pmatrix} = \begin{bmatrix} 1 & 0 & 0 \\ a_{21} & 1 & 0 \\ a_{31} & a_{32} & 1 \end{bmatrix} \times \begin{pmatrix} \varepsilon_{real\,activity\,shock} \\ \varepsilon_{financial\,stress\,shock} \\ \varepsilon_{monetary\,policy\,shock} \end{pmatrix} \qquad (7.3)$$

In the next step, we examine the impact of the identified structural shocks on Asia's stock prices (STP) by estimating OLS regressions. The explanatory variables are the three structural shocks identified previously, which are standardized by subtracting the mean and dividing by the standard deviation[e]. The sample includes data for seven Asian economies (Japan, China, Hong Kong, Taiwan, Korea, Singapore, and India). An OLS regression is estimated for each economy's benchmark stock market index using monthly data from 2000M1 to 2012M12[f].

The effects of the estimated structural shocks on the stock prices are estimated using the following regressions:

---

[e] STP is converted to the real value by deflating with the CPI. The data source used is the IMF's International Financial Statistics.

[f] A start date of 1991 reflects the need to accommodate lags in the VAR.

$$\Delta STP_t = \beta_j + \sum_{i=0}^{12} \tau_{ji}\hat{\varepsilon}_{jt-i} + v_{jt} \quad j = 1,2,3 \qquad (7.4)$$

where Δ denotes the percentage change in the STP, α_j, β_j, and γ_j are constant terms, φ_{ji}, τ_{ji}, and ω_{ji} are the impulse response coefficients at forecast horizon i, $\hat{\varepsilon}_{j,t}$ denotes the estimated j^{th} structural shock in the tth month, and r_{jt}, v_{jt} and s_{jt} are error terms. The maximum lag is determined by the maximum horizon of the impulse function, which is set to 12 months. To avoid serial correlation in the error terms, the block bootstrap method is used to infer the estimated coefficients. We use an overlapping moving block bootstrap method with block size 4 and 20,000 bootstrap replications.[g]

7.4   Estimation Results

The cumulative impulse responses of the STP to the structural shocks are shown in Figure 7.1. The dotted and dashed lines represent one-standard-error and two-standard-error bands, respectively. In the following discussion, the statistical significance is determined based on one-standard-error bands.

A positive real activity shock (i.e., an unexpected increase in US real economic activity) causes a statistically significant increase in the STP for some short horizons in all countries except in China. However, these cumulative STP responses peak after two or three months, followed by a statistically insignificant decline that fully offsets the initial increase. The result indicates that the impact of the real activity shock on the STP is not persistent.

A positive financial stress shock (i.e., an unexpected increase in US financial stress) causes a sustained and statistically significant decline in the STP in all countries. The cumulative responses of the STP are statistically significant for more than five months in all countries except in China. Even based on the two-standard-error bands, these cumulative responses are statistically significant for the first few months in Hong Kong, Taiwan, Korea, and India, and for more than four months in Japan

---

[g] See MacKinnon [2006] for a survey of bootstrapping methods.

and Singapore. The initial impact of this shock on the STP is largely sustained, and the cumulative responses remain negative after 12 months, which is more persistent that the effect of the real activity shock.

Interestingly, a positive monetary policy shock (i.e., an unexpected increase in the FF rate) has no statistically significant impact on the STP in all countries except in Hong Kong, Taiwan, and Korea, where US tightening of monetary policy causes a temporary and statistically significant decline in the STP at least initially. This result indicates that an unexpected change in the US monetary policy has little direct effects on Asian stock prices. As suggested by the credit-view of monetary policy transmission [Bernanke and Gertler, 1995], monetary policy operates through changes in funding costs and credit availability. Therefore, it is possible that the monetary policy shock is transmitted indirectly through the financial stress shock.

[India]

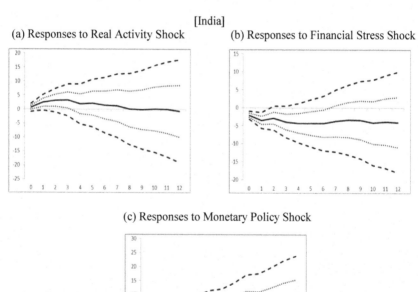

(a) Responses to Real Activity Shock   (b) Responses to Financial Stress Shock

(c) Responses to Monetary Policy Shock

Figure 7.1. Cumulative responses of Asian stock prices to US structural shocks.

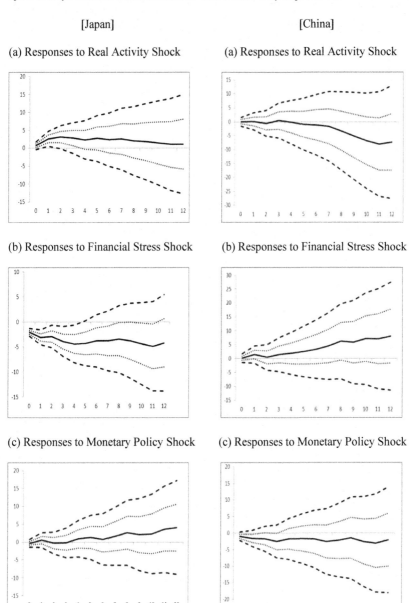

Figure 7.1. (*Continued*)

[Hong Kong]   [Taiwan]

(a) Responses to Real Activity Shock   (a) Responses to Real Activity Shock

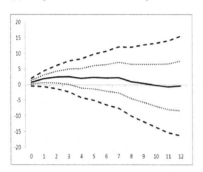   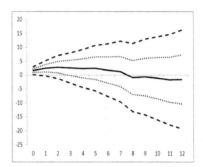

(b) Responses to Financial Stress Shock   (b) Responses to Financial Stress Shock

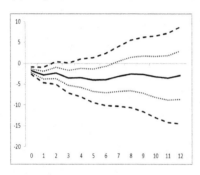   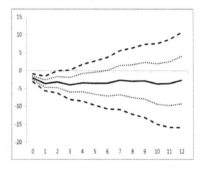

(c) Responses to Monetary Policy Shock   (c) Responses to Monetary Policy Shock

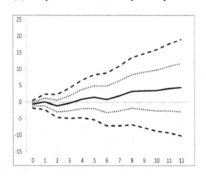   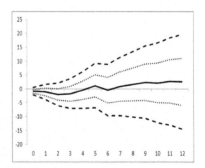

Figure 7.1. (*Continued*)

[Korea]   [Singapore]

(a) Responses to Real Activity Shock   (a) Responses to Real Activity Shock

(b) Responses to Financial Stress Shock   (b) Responses to Financial Stress Shock

(c) Responses to Monetary Policy Shock (c) Responses to Monetary Policy Shock

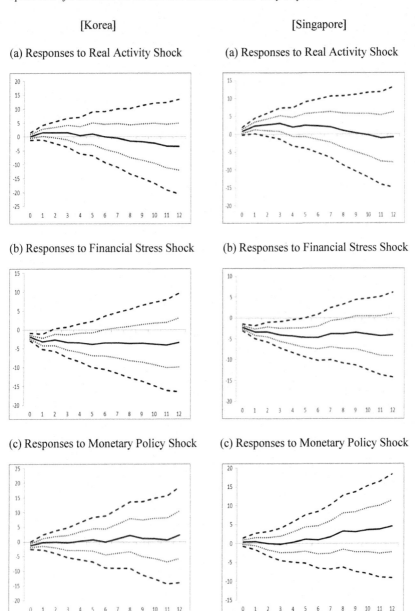

Figure 7.1. (*Continued*)

To summarize, the US financial stress shock has a statistically significant cross-border spillover effect on Asian stock prices. The impact on Asian stock prices of the US financial stress shock is more persistent than that of the US real activity shock. By contrast, the US monetary policy shock has little direct spillover effects on Asian stock prices, indicating the possibility that the monetary policy shock is transmitted indirectly through the financial stress shock.

7.5   Policy Implications

As the above analysis suggests, the spillover effects of financial stress could have different macroeconomic impacts in different countries. Therefore, financial reforms aimed at mitigating the adverse impact of financial spillover needs to be tailored in accordance with the underlying economic and financial structures that could affect the pattern of spillovers. At the same time, international efforts should be made to promote harmonization in financial regulations across jurisdictions. The presence of substantial inconsistency among national regulations could create incentives for financial institutions to seek regulatory arbitrage, moving their operations from heavily regulated jurisdictions to lightly regulated ones. Regulatory arbitrage would undermine the effectiveness of regulatory reforms and expose all relevant jurisdictions to the danger of excessive risk taking by imprudent banks due to their interconnected nature of business [Acharya, 2013].

In this context, Asian countries should cooperate closely to address a major loophole in financial regulations, namely, a lack of effective oversight and regulations of shadow banking systems. A narrow focus of financial reforms on banking sectors could create incentives for lending activities to migrate towards less regulated segments, notably shadow banking systems. A growth of shadow banking systems could jeopardize the stability of the entire financial system due to the interconnection between regulated and shadow-banking systems. From a broader perspective of macro-financial stability, financial regulators should develop an effective framework for oversight and regulations of shadow banking systems. Asian countries can cooperate to monitor the progress of the neighboring countries' reforms on shadow banking regulations. To this end, the scope of the existing framework for regional financial cooperation, notably the ASEAN plus three (China, Japan, and Korea) can be expanded.

It should, however, be emphasized that a lack of sufficient capacity is a major constraint for effective financial regulation and supervision. It is therefore essential for capacity-constraint countries to prioritize financial reforms and develop a long-term plan with an adequate sequencing of reforms. For example, in low-income countries with severe capacity constraints, the priority should be placed on financial stability. In these countries, financial liberalization must proceed gradually in tandem with the pace of capacity building. In middle-income countries, efforts should be made to remove regulatory barriers that restrain competition in banking sectors and hinder the price-discovery function of asset markets. Macroprudential measures, such as capital controls can be justified on a temporary basis to handle adverse external shocks, notably financial spillovers. However, capital controls cannot be a substitute for policy adjustments necessary to rectify macroeconomic and financial imbalances. It should also be noted that capital controls could have a detrimental effect on the development of financial systems in the long run [Chin and Ito, 2002]. To support the less developed countries' efforts to formulate a roadmap for financial reforms, Asia's advanced countries can share their experiences and develop a guideline for an adequate sequencing of reforms within the framework of ASEAN plus three.

7.6   Conclusions

This chapter examined the cross-border spillovers of US financial stress shocks on Asian stock markets. Financial stress seriously disrupts normal financial market functioning and is associated with greater asset price volatility, higher funding costs, and the reduced bank credit availability. Financial stress can adversely affect real economic activity by depressing corporate and household spending. Moreover, financial stress in one country can be transmitted to foreign countries through various channels, exerting cross-border spillover effects on their financial markets, including stock markets.

To examine the cross-border spillovers of the US financial stress shock, we followed Kilian's [2009] two-step procedure. First, a VAR was estimated to identify structural shocks. Next, OLS regressions were estimated to evaluate the impact of identified structural shocks on the stock prices in seven Asian economies. We have found that the US financial stress shock has a statistically significant cross-border spillover effect on Asian stock prices. The impact on Asian stock prices of the US financial stress shock is more persistent than that of the US real activity shock. By contrast, the US monetary policy shock has little direct spillover effects on Asian stock prices, indicating the possibility that the monetary policy shock is transmitted indirectly through the financial stress shock.

Key policy implications derived from the analysis are two-fold. First, Asian countries should cooperate closely to address a major loophole in financial regulations, particularly, a lack of effective oversight and regulations of shadow-banking systems. Second, to support the less developed countries' efforts to formulate a roadmap for financial reforms, Asia's advanced countries can share their experiences and develop a guideline for an adequate sequencing of reforms. To these ends, the scope of the existing framework for regional financial cooperation, notably the ASEAN plus three can be expanded.

References

Apergis, N. and Miller, S.M. (2009). Do structural oil-market shocks affect stock prices? *Energy Economics*, 31, pp. 569–575.

Acharya, V.V. (2013) *New paradigms for financial regulations: emerging market perspectives*, eds. Kawai, M. and Prasad, E.S., "The Dodd-Frank Act and Basel III: intentions, unintended consequences, and lessons for emerging markets," (Tokyo and Brookings Institution Press, Washington DC) pp. 13–44.

Artis, M.J., Galvao, A.B. and Marcellino, M. (2007). The transmission mechanism in a changing world, *Journal of Applied Econometrics*, 22, pp. 39–61.

Bernanke, B.S. and Gertler, M. (1995). Inside the black box: the credit channel of monetary policy transmission, *Journal of Economic Perspectives*, 9(1), pp. 27–48.

Bernanke, B.S., Boivin, J. and Eliasz, P. (2005). Measuring the effects of monetary policy: a factor-augmented vector autoregressive (FVAR) approach, *Quarterly Journal of Economics*, February, pp. 387–422.

Canova, F. (2005). The transmission of US shocks to Latin America, *Journal of Applied Econometrics*, 20, pp. 229–251.

Cerra, V. and Saxena, S. (2008). Growth dynamics: The myth of economic recovery, *American Economic Review*, 98, pp. 439–457.

Chen, W., Hamori, S. and Kinkyo, T. (2014). Macroeconomic impacts of oil prices and underlying financial shocks, *Journal of International Financial Markets, Institutions, and Money*, 29, pp. 1–12.

Chin, M. and Ito, H. (2002). Capital account liberalization, institutions and financial development: cross country evidence, *NBER Working Papers*, 8967.

Eichengreen, B., Rose, A. and Wyplosz, C. (1996). Contagious currency crises: First tests, *Scandinavian Journal of Economics*, 98, pp. 463–484.

Forbes, K.J. (2012) The "Big C": identifying and mitigating contagion, Paper prepared for 2012 Jackson Hole Symposium hosted by the Federal Reserve Bank of Kansas City.

FSB (2013). Strengthening oversight and regulation of shadow banking: policy framework for strengthening oversight and regulation of shadow banking entities, Financial Stability Board, Basel.

Fornari, F. and Stracca, L. (2012). What does a financial shock do? First international evidence, *Economic Policy*, July, pp. 407–445.

Galesi, A. and Sgherri, S. (2009). Regional financial spillovers across Europe: a global VAR analysis, *IMF Working Paper*, WP/09/23.

Gelos, G. (2011). International mutual funds, capital flow volatility, and contagion — A survey, *IMF Working Paper*, WP/11/92.

Goldstein, M. (1998). The Asian financial crisis: causes, curses, and systematic implications, Institute for International Economics, Washington DC.

Hakkio, C.S. and Keeton, W.R. (2009). Financial stress: what is it, how can it be measured, and why does it matter? Federal Reserve Bank of Kansas City, *Economic Review*, Second Quarter.

Hanson, S.G., Kashyap, A.K. and Stein, J.C. (2011). A macroprudential approach to financial regulation, *Journal of Economic Perspectives*, 25, pp. 3–28.

Helbling, T., Huidrom, R., Kose, M.A. and Otrok, C. (2011). Do credit shocks matter? A global perspective, *European Economic Review*, 55, pp. 340–353.

IMF (2009). Regional economic outlook: Asia and Pacific, International Monetary Fund, Washington DC, May.

IMF (2013). Dancing together? Spillovers, common shocks, and the role of financial and trade linkages, *World Economic Outlook*, October 2013, Chapter 3. International Monetary Fund, Washington DC.

Kaminsky, G. and Reinhaart, C. (2000). On crises, contagion, and confusion, *Journal of International Economics*, 51, pp. 145–168.

Kilian, L. (2009). Not all oil price shocks are alike: disentangling demand and supply shocks in the crude oil market, *American Economic Review*, 99, pp. 1053–1069.

Kilian, L. and Park, C. (2009). The impact of oil price shocks on the US stock market, *International Economic Review*, 50, pp. 1267–1287.

Kim, S. (2001). International Transmission of US monetary policy shocks: evidence from VARs, *Journal of Monetary Economics*, 48, 339–372.

MacKinnon, J.G. (2006). Bootstrap methods in econometrics, *Economic Record*, 82, pp. 2–18.

Mackowiak, B. (2007). External shocks, U.S. monetary policy and macroeconomic fluctuations in emerging markets, *Journal of Monetary Economics*, 54, pp. 2512–2520.

Mumtaz, H.P. and Surico, P. (2009). The transmission of international shocks: a factor-augmented VAR approach, *Journal of Money, Credit, and Banking*, 41, pp. 71–100.

Neri, S. and Nobili, A. (2010). The transmission of US monetary policy to the euro area, *International Finance*, 13, pp. 55–78.

Raddatz, C. and Schmukler, S. (2012). On the international transmission of shocks: micro-evidence from mutual fund portfolios, *Journal of International Economics*, 88, pp. 357–374.

Reinhart, C. and Rogoff, K. (2009). *This Time Is Different: Eight Centuries of Financial Folly*, (Princeton University Press, Princeton).

Yoshizaki, Y. and Hamori, S. (2013). On the influence of oil price shocks on economic activity, inflation, and exchange rates, *International Journal of Financial Research*, 4, pp. 33–41.

Chapter 8

Challenges to Macroeconomic Management in Resource-Rich Developing Economies

Kazue Demachi

Graduate School of International Cooperation Studies, Kobe University

2-1, Rokkodai-cho, Nada-Ku, Kobe 657-8501 Hyogo, Japan

Email: k.demachi@people.kobe-u.ac.jp

Takuji Kinkyo

Faculty of Economics, Kobe University

2-1, Rokkodai-cho, Nada-Ku, Kobe, 657-8501 Hyogo, Japan

Email: kinkyo@econ.kobe-u.ac.jp

8.1 Introduction

Recent high natural resource prices have attracted increasing FDI inflows into resource-rich Developing Economies (RRDEs). Resource-rich countries in Sub-Saharan Africa and Asia, which have suffered from long-term economic stagnation, are now rapidly expanding their economies. Natural resource exports, however, not only lead to greater export earnings but also cause many problems in RRDEs. Rapid economic expansion led by natural resource exports and high prices often result in a consumption boom but less investment into the development of economic and social infrastructure in exporting countries, whereas foreign direct investment into extractive industries does not generate many employment opportunities in economies already suffering from high unemployment. Natural resource price development and fluctuations in international markets especially complicate RRDE governments' ability to stabilize their macro economies. This chapter reviews and discusses the issues and stylized facts on resource revenue management and macroeconomic stabilization in RRDEs.

8.2 Problems Facing RRDEs

8.2.1 *Resource curse*

Natural resource discoveries or price increases are a "blessing" for a developing country, especially when the resulting resource revenues fill the government's revenue gap through abundant foreign currency. However, the sheer amount of foreign currency earnings as well as the unstable nature of the inflows induce a number of problems, which are exacerbated by institutional weakness or low government capacity. The paradoxical situation of RRDEs is often discussed as a "resource curse," because despite this source of wealth, they have experienced slower growth, unstable macro economies, or domestic conflicts.

Economic analyses on the resource curse cover a wide scope. Gelb *et al.* [1988] comprehensively analyzed the economies of oil-producing countries after the oil price hikes in the 1970s and suggested various problems due to oil windfall inflows, and the boom and bust cycle. Auty [1990] highlighted the difficulties and risks for developing countries in promoting resource-based industrialization. Sachs and Warner [2001] use a cross-country analysis to reveal the slower economic growth rate of countries that are highly dependent on natural resource exports. On the other hand, Collier and Hoeffler [2000] argue that the possibility of gaining natural resource revenue increases a country's conflict risk and prolongs the conflicts that arise. Karl [1997] discusses how opportunities to access the rents associated with natural resources tend to induce governmental corruption and Ross [2012] argues that societies whose economies depend on crude oil exports tend to be undemocratic with lower female status in their societies. Analyses on Dutch disease, changes in domestic resource allocation and production structure, can also be categorized as falling within the scope of the resource curse argument [Corden and Neary, 1982; Corden, 1984; Cuddington, 1989; Van der Ploeg and Venables, 2013].

Resource price movements are affected by economic as well as geopolitical factors, and their high volatility and uncertainty in turn negatively affect national budgets and economies of resource exporting countries. Analysis of international resource price volatility is gaining importance. For RRDEs to manage their resource revenue and stabilize their macro economies, buffering their economy from the risks of price volatility is a critical task.

8.2.2 *Volatility and uncertainty of international resource prices*

Natural resource prices in international markets are highly volatile. Among others, crude oil's price reflects various international economic factors, and its price movements also strongly influence both oil consumers and producers [Apergis and Miller, 2009; Hamilton, 1983; 1996; 2003; 2008; Kilian, 2009; Kim and Roubini, 2000; Chen *et al.*, 2013].

Economies dependent on natural resource revenue have to face the possibility of radical changes in revenue due to price movements, whereas difficulties in forecasting price movements lead to current account deficits, debt accumulations, and exchange rate problems. The root cause of RRDEs' problems lies in the procyclical nature of their policies formulated under weak institutions. These procyclical policies, namely, budget expansions in boom periods and austerity when prices fall, exacerbates the influence of price movements. Moreover, tightening government expenditures is often complicated due to multiyear investment planning, or resistance to reducing the number of government sector employees [Frankel, 2011a]. Governmental attempts to smooth its intertemporal consumption by borrowing in the downturn and repaying in the boom seem reasonable. However, in the 1980s, the debt incurred by RRDE governments to fill the "temporal" revenue gap turned into a debt accumulation problem. In this scenario, establishing a natural resource fund is suggested as an effective policy tool to enable countercyclical macroeconomic management in RRDEs

8.3   The Role of Fiscal Policy for Inclusive Growth

Nonrenewable resources, regardless of type and level of endowment, will someday dry up. Hoteling [1931] discusses the optimal timing and pace of extracting limited resources, which has attracted the interest of many economists, including Solow [1974] and Stiglitz [1974] during the oil crisis in the 1970s. Recent increases in international demand for natural resources and their resulting price hikes have led to renewed attention on this issue. On the other hand, international society has been converging on the view that economic development should feature "inclusive growth."[a] This view suggests that RRDEs' economic growth should also be inclusive, allocating natural resource revenue to narrow domestic income gaps and alleviate economic inequalities. To achieve inclusive growth, effective reallocation of natural resource revenue is expected through policies including promotion of the private sector, which leads to new job creation, the development of the agricultural sector with investment in rural infrastructure, and investment in basic social services such as health care and sanitation. RRDEs are also required to develop alternative industries to resource extraction, since extractive industries is basically highly capital intensive and create few jobs, while poverty reduction needs to be achieved by offering job opportunities to a wider range of people [Auty, 2001].

---

[a] The definition of Inclusive Growth is discussed by The Economic Policy and Debt Department of the World Bank [PRMED, 2009]. The UN System Task Team [2012] also examines Inclusive Growth as an alternative of post-MDG development philosophy.

To activate policies to promote inclusive growth, proper governmental management of natural resource revenue is critical. One policy tool particularly recommended for RRDEs to achieve this aim is the Natural Resource Fund (NRF).

8.3.1 *Natural resource fund*

The NRF's aims as well as its name differ across countries. The core three functions of the NRF are economic stabilization against price movements, saving for future generations, and funding economic and social development [IMF, 2012]. Among these, the first function seeks to buffer against fluctuation of resource revenue flows to stabilize the government's budget and macro economy. This postulates that resource revenue is consumed by the current generation. On the other hand, the remaining functions object to retaining the wealth gained from natural resource sales as man-made capital or socio-economic assets in favor of transferring them to future generations. This adds weight to the fair allocation of wealth between generations, wherein preserving asset values is critical. Depending on which function is prioritized, the fund management approach also changes.

These NRFs are regarded as Sovereign Wealth Funds (SWF) as long as they are managed by central or regional governments and invested internationally and strategically[b]. SWFs have been established in many countries including non-resource countries. The International Working Group of Sovereign Wealth Funds (IWG) was established in 2008, and formed an agreement called the "Santiago Principles" [IWG, 2008]. In 2009, IWG established the International Forum of Sovereign Wealth Funds (IFSWF). A total of 25 countries currently participate, some participants are resource-rich countries. However, those engaging in

---

[b] IWG defines SWFs as "special purpose investment funds or arrangements, owned by the general government...investing in foreign financial assets.... The SWFs are commonly established out of balance of payments surpluses, official foreign currency operations, the proceeds of privatizations, fiscal surpluses, and /or receipts resulting from commodity export" [IWG, 2008: 27].

strategic investing are the ones with relatively high government capacity, such as Norway, Kuwait, Oman, Botswana, and Chile.

Considering NWFs as a policy tool for macroeconomic management in RRDEs, the tasks of resource revenue management arise in two different time frames: dealing with high price volatility and stabilizing the macro economy in the short- and medium-term, and sustaining the revenue from limited and unrenewable resources in the long-term.

8.3.2 *Managing short- and medium-term price volatility*

International society has accumulated knowledge regarding effective policy tools to prevent the boom and bust cycles experienced in many resource-rich countries in the 1970s and 80s. The International Monetary Fund (IMF) recommends resource-rich countries to establish a Stabilization Fund, that is, an NRF especially intended to insulate the macro economy from price shocks and uncertainty [Davis *et al.*, 2001]. A Stabilization Fund functions by accumulating government savings when the resource price is above the benchmark, which is then withdrawn when the price falls below the benchmark. Some oil producers, such as Kuwait, established this type of fund in the early phase of their oil production; however, the most renowned is Chile's Copper Stabilization Fund and the countercyclical fiscal policy pursued by the Chilean government (Table 8.1).

In Chile, two panels of specialists are set up to analyze the copper price to form a medium-term fiscal policy that enables the government to control over-expending during booms and offers disbursement to stimulate the economy in economic downturns [Frankel, 2011b; IMF, 2012]. While Chile's success in resource revenue management can be a model for other RRDEs, setting up expert panels independent from political pressure is not viable in many cases for RRDE with weak institutions. Moreover, Chile's success is due to the government's voluntary commitment to a countercyclical policy.

The effect of establishing such a fund should not be exaggerated. The setting up of a fund itself does not prevent illegal acquisition and dispersion of resource wealth through corruption, since it does not directly affect governmental activities and judgments in the budgetary process.

Table 8.1. Names and objectives of Natural Resource Fund of selected countries.

Country	Funding	Fund name Object	Resource
Alberta (Canada)	1976	*Alberta Heritage Savings Trust Fund* Saving, economic, and social development	Oil and Gas
Alaska (United States)	1976	*Alaska Permanent Fund* Saving	Oil
Chile[1] (activated in 1987)	1985	*Copper Stabilization Fund** Saving	Copper
	2007	*Economic and Social Stabilization Fund** Saving	
Kuwait	1960	*General Reserve Fund* Stabilization and saving	Oil
	1976	*Future Generation Fund* Saving	
Kiribati[2]	1956	*Revenue Equalization Reserve Fund* Stabilization and saving	Phosphate
Norway (activated in 1995)	1990	*State Petroleum Fund* Stabilization and saving	Oil
Oman[3]	1980	*State General Reserve Fund* Saving	Oil
	1993	*Oil Fund** Investment in oil sector	
	2006	*Oman Investment Fund** Domestic and foreign investment	
Papua New Guinea (wound up in 2001)	1974	*Mineral Resources Stabilization Fund* Stabilization	Minerals
Azerbaijan	1999	*State Oil Fund* Saving	Oil and Gas
Botswana	1993	*Pula Fund* Saving	Diamond

Notes: [1]Ministry of Finance, Chile HP (http://www.hacienda.cl/english/ sovereignn-wealth-funds/economic-and-social-stabilization-fund.html, last accessed on May 27, 2014). [2]Phosphate stock exhausted in 1979. [3]Sovereign Wealth Fund Institute HP (http://www.swfinstitute.org/swfs/oif/, last accessed on May 27, 2014). *integrated into new fund due to change in objectives and concerned laws.
Sources: Davis *et al.* [2001] Table 3.1 and IWG [2008], except for Chile and Oman.

For example, Nigeria, having problems in oil management, established NRFs but fund resources were illegally withdrawn. Another limitation of Stabilization Funds is that such large scale funds need to be managed outside the country to insulate the economy from price movement shocks. Thus, the strict operation of a Stabilization Fund means that resource-scare RRDEs in need of capital cannot benefit from current natural resource revenue.

The establishment of a Stabilization Fund is clearly not a panacea for RRDEs with weak institutions. The dilemma that "NRFs are least needed when institutions are strong; but they are least likely to work in precisely those institutionally weak environments where they appear to be most needed" is now widely acknowledged [Humphreys and Sandbu, 2007: 226]. Reflecting this point, increasing international support for RRDEs is offered for government capacity development and institutional quality improvements. The IMF also implements training for capacity building in resource management for RRDEs [IMF, 2012].

8.3.3 Long-term fiscal sustainability

Exporting non-renewable natural resources to gain revenue is now regarded as transforming a natural underground national asset into a manmade asset. National assets need to be managed to equally benefit not only the current but future generations. Sustaining natural resource revenue as a national asset thus becomes a focus of resource management. A basic approach to this purpose can be constructed on the basis of Friedman's permanent income hypothesis [Barnet and Ossowski, 2002; IMF, 2012]. According to this hypothesis, revenue from non-renewable resources is regarded as transitory income, and the consumption by governments and people in resource-rich countries needs to be based on the permanent income earned from non-resource production. As transitory income, resource revenue needs to be saved first, and its consumption need to be distributed over the long run, across generations beyond the resource's exhaustion.

This approach reflects past experiences of RRDEs during the 1970s and 80s. Governments at that time had insufficient fiscal management capacity, incapable of making the right decisions when choosing projects for investment, and also lacking capacity in terms of project evaluation, which resulted in rapid, substantial, and ineffective investments into a domestic economy having low absorption capacities. As a result, a large proportion of resource revenue was wasted on incomplete projects, or dispersed through inappropriate consumption and corruption. RRDEs today are counseled not to invest resource revenue into the domestic economy, but set it aside as foreign reserves until domestic absorption capacity can be sufficiently developed. Moreover, to leave sufficient assets for the future generation, the current population is urged to consume or invest only the interest gained from the NRF's management. On the basis of this point, the IMF recommends that resource-rich countries distinguish resource revenue from other government revenue [Leigh and Olters, 2006]. Norway is often named as a success case of resource fund management based on such a very careful and sustainable asset management (bird-in-hand) approach, which consumes only secure investment profit earned through NRF management. This oil-producing country invests its oil revenue into its national pension fund, and the pension fund's profits are integrated into government revenue. The non-oil budget account is distinguished from the oil account, and the budget deficit is controlled so as not to exceed the amount of the investment profit gained from the national pension fund [Norwegian Ministry of Finance, 2014].

The idea that fiscal management should be based on non-resource revenue is rational in countries like Norway, with good institutions, a mature government capacity, transparency, and a developed domestic economy. This approach, however, is not realistic for most RRDEs, who suffer from the so-called "resource curse," since it means giving up current poverty reduction programs and improvements in living conditions in favor of future generations' welfare. Moreover, it has been suggested that the permanent income hypothesis is a theory of consumption, but investments must be also taken into consideration in the context of RRDEs [IMF, 2012].

A number of analyses have already discussed alternative theoretical bases to support large-scale current consumption and investment using natural resource revenue. Takizawa *et al.* [2004] analyzed how consumption levels at steady-state vary depending on the timing of resource revenue consumption. According to their analysis, increases in current public expenditure will lead to higher private investment, and the current generation's consumption level will rise. However, as capital's profitability declines with time, future generations will find that their consumption level is lower than the case where resource revenue consumption is distributed over generations based on the permanent income hypothesis. On the other hand, Sachs [2007] argues that resource revenue in RRDEs should be invested in domestic economies. He mentions that associated concerns such as the Dutch disease will not be a problem as long as public expenditures are allocated not to consumption but investment. Collier *et al.* [2010] also argue that RRDEs should invest resource revenue into the capital-scarce domestic economy, or pay back current debt, rather than accumulating revenue outside the country and postpone the benefits to far future. They especially mention the importance of RRDEs keeping public investments high.

Reflecting these arguments, the policies recommended to countries particularly suffering from weak institutions and facing credit constraints, such as resource-rich Sub-Saharan countries, add weight on balancing current accounts rather than achieving fiscal sustainability. This approach uses Stabilization Funds as a political tool, and enables the governments to consume and invest resource revenue when there is excess of such revenue [IMF, 2012]. Such policies have the goal of macroeconomic stabilization in the short- and medium-term, but not long-term economic stabilization. On this point, the problem reflects recurrent issues associated with governmental actions and decisions. Policy success strongly depends on government decisions regarding field to target for investment and promotion of economic development. To evaluate investment projects and determine their scales, the IMF offers several indices and rules, but improvements in government capacity and institutional quality remain the most critical tasks.

8.3.4 *Sustainability in different forms*

The discussion above is based on the assumption that national wealth from natural resources is converted into capital assets, but national assets can take other forms, including human or social capital. Collier suggests

RRDEs learn from the experiences of middle-income countries such as Indonesia and Malaysia in terms of their resource management, rather than from Norway [Collier, 2010]. Indonesia and Malaysia benefited from exports of their rich natural resources in the early phase of their economic development, but escaped the resource curse, achieved industrialization, and promoted agricultural development by utilizing resource revenue to realize sustainable development.

In the 1970s, paralleled with the Green Revolution, Indonesia allocated oil revenue into rural infrastructure, investments in irrigation, and rural development [Auty, 1990]. The Indonesian government also used oil revenue to implement large-scale projects to build 61,000 schools in 1973–74 and 1978–79. Duflo [2001] determined that this school project had positive effects on the enrolment ratio, and local wages benefited from this project. Investment in schools and education can be regarded as establishment of sustainable assets in forms of social infrastructure and human capital. In terms of inclusive growth, this school project enabled unenrolled children in poor households to receive education through reallocation of natural resource revenue, which eventually lead to long-term poverty reduction.

Malaysia, on the other hand, achieved "resource-based industrialization" by allocating natural resource revenue into investment in heavy industries [Auty, 1990]. The development of domestic manufacturing industries, such as electronics, is also meaningful for inclusive growth and job creation. Approximately 30% of Malaysian government revenue today is derived from the tax revenue and dividend paid by the national oil company, Petronas. In the 1970s, 80% of Petonas's payment was oil sales tax, but as the company grew and its operations became profitable, its net profits and dividend amounted to 45% of its payment to the government in 2007. In 2008, reflecting international oil price increases, Petronas made a special payment equivalent to US$ 18 billion to the government [Yusof, 2011]. As some national oil companies such as Statoil or Norway expand their operations beyond their home countries, Petronas also invests in foreign projects, expanding its activity into the international sphere. Malaysian resource management can be regarded as a process that converted national assets in the form of crude oil and natural gas into a corporation that sustainably produces profits.

8.4 Conclusions

The political tools mentioned above postulate certain levels of governmental capacity. However, the institutions and governmental capacities of RRDEs are yet to be improved, and their capacity development is especially required for effective resource revenue allocation. Enhancing transparency of revenue from natural resources

Table 8.2. Debt stock of selected RRDEs.

	Natural resource rent (2012)[1]	GDP growth rate 2003-2012 (%)	Debt stock (share of export, 2012)[2]	Debt stock (share of GNI)	Share of concessional loans
Angola	42.62	10.81	30.74	21.60	19.92
Azerbaijan	39.77	13.47	25.67	16.31	27.32
Burkina Faso	14.86	6.18	109.72*	23.97	87.04
Congo, D.R.	27.66	6.23	63.93	35.76	49.86
Ghana	13.95	7.29	73.77	32.25	47.10
Kazakhstan	29.51	7.25	138.54	78.98	0.80
Laos	13.56	7.58	218.43	73.44	40.73
Mauritania	47.15	6.01	114.90	82.34	69.59
Mongol	14.07	8.75	94.05	52.96	34.18
Nigeria	28.68	9.50	10.17	4.21	59.19
Peru	10.99	6.52	105.73	29.36	7.08
Zambia	20.12	6.21	54.44	27.56	39.95

Notes: [1]Sum of oil, natural gas, mineral rents. Natural resource rents are calculated as the difference between international price and production cost multiplied by the quantity of extraction. For detailed definition, see the metadata of *World Development Indicators*.
[2]External debt stocks (% of exports of goods, services and primary income).
* Data of year 2010.
Sources: World Bank [2014].

and its expenditure is also a critical issue facing RRDE governments and citizens. The Extractive Industry Transparency Initiative (EITI), an international initiative, supports the management of natural resource revenue, especially in RRDEs[c]. Some governments employ the EITI scheme to obtain information on unknown real resource revenue figures, such as the Myanmar government, who committed itself to implementation of EITI as a neutral tool to control resource revenue, which is strongly influenced by the state-owned corporation.

On the other hand, RRDE debts are a critical issue not only for their own economies but also for international society. More than a few RRDEs have experienced debt problems and subsequent economic stagnation as a result of excess borrowing during economic boom and bust cycles due to radical fluctuations of resource prices in the 1970s and 80s. Recently, however, some RRDEs seem to be repeating past experiences. Table 8.2 shows the debt stock of selected RRDEs for whom the economic growth rate is quite high (more than 6% annual average between 2003 and 2012) and the dependency on natural resource revenue (natural resource rent) in 2012 is more than 10%.

As shown in the table, Kazakhstan is in a typical Dutch disease situation, and as the economy was hit by the international financial crisis, loans directed to real estate became nonperforming. The large part of capital inflows are financed through international financial markets. Laos, on the other hand, is growing rapidly thanks to natural gas extraction, but so is its debt stock. The Democratic Republic of Congo (DRC) and Zambia had very high debt ratios. The DRC's debt stock substantially reduced in 2010, whereas Zambia's fell during 2003 and 2006, and their debt stock in 2012 is not alarmingly high. However, their reduction of debt stock is the result of debt cancelation by aid donor countries based on the Debt Relief Initiative for Highly Indebted Poor Countries, and not necessarily reflective of high economic performance or sound public finance management [IMF, 2005; World Bank, 2010].

Furthermore, many other countries can be considered "would-be" RRDEs. The natural resource rent share in their economies is not yet very high, but increasing amounts of FDI are flowing into the exploration

---

[c] EITI web site, http://eiti.org/ [accessed on May 30, 2014].

and development of natural resources. Tanzania, Kenya, Ethiopia, and other countries in Sub-Saharan Africa are expected to produce more natural resources, while in South East Asia, Myanmar's natural gas exports are also growing. These countries also need to be cautious against over-borrowing and debt accumulation.

In most poor countries, whether resource-rich or not, weak institutions are both the result and cause of poverty, and governments face difficulties in macroeconomic management. The existence of natural resources, however, complicates their problems. Governments of resource-rich countries are required to understand the problems associated with revenue management, and avoid repeating the failures of past RRDEs. Recent high international resource prices bring the prospect of resource-booms in RRDEs, and such booms often mask fundamental problems such as weak institutions and unsound fiscal management. In addition, the so-called "resource curse" can reappear once resource prices decrease, and its cost is substantial. Accordingly, institutionalization of sound resource management and economic diversification should be prioritized.

References

Apergis, N. and Miller, S. M. (2009). Do Structural Oil-market Shocks Affect Stock Prices? *Energy Economics,* 31, pp. 169–171.

Auty, R. (1990). *Resource-Based Industrialization* (Clarendon Press, Oxford).

Auty, R. (2001). The Political Economy of Resource-driven Growth, *European Economic Review,* 45, pp. 839–846.

Barnet, S. and Ossowski, R. (2002). Operational Aspects of Fiscal Policy in Oil-Producing Countries, *IMF Working Paper* WP/02/177.

Chen, W., Hamori, S. and Kinkyo, T. (2014). Macroeconomic Impacts of Oil Prices and Underlying Financial Shocks, *Journal of International Financial Markets, Institutions and Money,* 29, pp. 1–12.

Collier, P. (2010). *Plundered Planet* (Oxford University Press, New York).

Collier, P. and Hoeffler, A. (2000). Greed and Grievance in Civil War, *Policy Research Working Paper* 2355, The World Bank.

Collier, P., Van Der Ploeg, R., Spence, M. and Venables, A. J. (2010). Managing Resource Revenues in Developing Economies, *IMF Staff Papers,* 57(1), pp. 84–118.

Corden, M. W. (1984). Booming Sector and Dutch Disease Economics: Survey and Consolidation, *Oxford Economic Papers,* New Series 36(3), pp. 359–380.

Corden, M. W. and Neary, J. P. (1982). Booming Sector and De-Industrialisation in a Small Open Economy, *The Economic Journal,* 92, pp. 825–848.

Cuddington, J. T. (1989). Commodity Export Booms in Developing Countries, *The World Bank Research Observer,* 4(2), pp. 143–165.

Daviś, J., Ossowski, R., Daniel, J. and Barnett, S. (2001). Stabilization and Saving Funds for Nonrenewable Resources: Experience and Fiscal Policy Implications, *IMF Occasional Paper* 205, International Monetary Fund.

Duflo, E. (2001). Schooling and Labor Market Consequences of School Construction in Indonesia: Evidence from an Unusual Policy Experiment, *The American Economic Review,* 91(4), pp. 795–813.

Frankel, J. A. (2011a). The Natural Resource Curse: A Survey, *NBER Working Paper* No. 15836.

Frankel, J. A. (2011b). A Solution to Fiscal Procyclicality: The Structural Budget Institutions Pioneered by Chile, *NBER Working Paper* No. 16945.

Gelb, A. and associates (1988). *Oil Windfalls: Blessing or Curse?* (Oxford University Press, New York).

Hamilton, J. D. (1983). Oil and the Macroeconomy since World War II, *Journal of Political Economy,* 91(2), pp. 228–248.

Hamilton, J. D. (1996). This is What Happened to the Oil Price-Macroeconomy Relationship, *Journal of Monetary Economics,* 38, pp. 215–220.

Hamilton, J. D. (2003). What is an Oil Shock? *Journal of Econometrics,* 113, pp. 363–398.

Hamilton, J. D. (2008). Understanding Crude Oil Price, *NBER Working Paper* 14492.

Hotelling, H. (1931). The Economics of Exhaustible Resources, *The Journal of Political Economy,* 39(2), pp. 137–175.

Humphreys, M. and Sandbu, M. E. (2007). The Political Economy of Natural Resource Fund, in M. Hamphreys, Sachs, J. D. and Stiglitz, J. E. Eds., *Escaping the Resource Curse* (Columbia University Press, New York), pp. 194–233.

IMF (2005). IMF and World Bank Support US$3.90 Billion in Debt Service Relief for Zambia. *Press Release* No.05/80, April 8, 2005, International Monetary Fund, http://www.imf.org/external/np/sec/pr/2005/pr0580.htm (Accessed on May 27, 2014).

IMF (2012). Macroeconomic Policy Frameworks for Resource-Rich Developing Countries. International Monetary Fund, http://www.imf.org/external/np/pp/eng/2012/082412.pdf (Accessed on May 19, 2014).

IWG (2008). Sovereign Wealth Funds: Generally Accepted Principles and Practices, "Santiago Principles." International Working Group of Sovereign Wealth Funds, http://www.iwg-swf.org/pubs/gapplist.htm (Accessed on May 23, 2014).

Karl, T. L. (1997). *Paradox of Plenty* (University of California Press, Berkeley and Los Angeles).

Kilian, L. (2009). Not All Oil Price Shocks Are Alike: Disentangling Demand and Supply Shocks in the Crude Oil Market, *American Economic Review*, 99(3), pp. 1053–1069.

Kim, S. and Roubini, N. (2000). Exchange Rate Anomalies in the Industrial Countries: A solution with a Structural VAR Approach, *Journal of Monetary Economics*, 45, pp. 561–586.

Leigh, D. and Olters, J. P. (2006). Natural-Resource Depletion, Habit Formation, and Sustainable Fiscal Policy: Lessons from Gabon, *IMF Working Paper* WP/06/193.

Norwegian Ministry of Finance (2014). The National Budget 2014: A Summary, Det Kongelige Finansdepartement, http://www.statsbudsjettet.no/Statsbudsjettet-2014/ English/ (Accessed on May 20, 2014).

PRMED (2009). What is Inclusive Growth? PRMED Knowledge Brief. The Economic Policy and Debt Department, The World Bank, http://go.worldbank.org/677R9R6 5J0 (Accessed on May 30, 2014).

Ross, M. (2012). *The Oil Curse* (Princeton University Press, Princeton).

Sachs, J. D. (2007). How to Handle the Macroeconomics of Oil Wealth, in Hamphreys, M., Sachs, J. D., and Stiglitz, J. E. Eds., *Escaping the Resource Curse* (Columbia University Press, New York), pp. 173–193.

Sachs, J. D. and Warner, A. W. (2001). The Curse of Natural Resources, *European Economic Review*, 45, pp. 827–838.

Solow, R. M. (1974). The Economics of Resources or the Resources of Economics, *The American Economic Review*, 64(2), pp. 1–14.

Stiglitz, J. E. (1974). Growth with Exhaustible Natural Resources: Efficient and Optimal Growth Paths, *Review of Economic Studies*, 42, pp. 123–137.

Takizawa, H., Gardner, E. H. and Ueda, K. (2004). Are Developing Countries Better Off Spending Their Oil Wealth Upfront? *IMF Working Paper* WP/04/141.

UN System Task Team (2012). *UN System Task Team on the Post-2015 UN Development Agenda*, UN System Task Team, http://www.un.org/millenniumgoals/pdf/ Think%20Pieces/12_macroeconomics.pdf (Accessed on May 30, 2014).

Van der Ploeg, F. and Venables, A. J. (2013). Absorbing a Windfall of Foreign Exchange: Dutch disease dynamics, *OxCarre Research Paper* 52, Oxford Center for the Analysis of Resource Rich Economies.

World Bank (2010). Congo — Enhanced Heavily Indebted Poor Countries (HIPC) Initiatives and the Multilateral Debt Relief Initiative (MDRI). World Bank, http://documents.worldbank.org/curated/en/2010/01/11636800/congo-enhanced-heavily-indebted-poor-countries-hipc-initiatives-multilateral-debt-relief-initiative-mdri (Accessed on May 27, 2014).

World Bank (2014). *World Development Indicators*, web database, http://databank.world-bank.org/data/databases.aspx (Accessed on May 23, 2014).

Yusof, Z. A. (2011). The Developmental State: Malaysia, in Collier, P. and Venables, A. J. Eds., *Plundered Nations? Successes and Failures in Natural Resource Extraction* (Palgrave Macmillan, Hampshire and New York), pp. 188–230.

Chapter 9

Policies and Prospects of ASEAN Financial Integration[a]

Satoshi Shimizu

Senior Economist

Economics Department, The Japan Research Institute, Limited

2-18-1 Higashigotanda, Shinagawa-ku, Tokyo 141-0022, Japan

Email: shimizu.satoshi@jri.co.jp

9.1 Introduction

Capital flows into developing countries in Asia and other regions have expanded rapidly in recent years. In addition to the benefits that these capital flows have brought, there have also been significant negative consequences, including increased public and private sector debt, and greater volatility in capital flows. In May 2013, indications that the United States was about to change its quantitative easing policy triggered a shift in capital inflows into developing countries, which had previously been expanding rapidly. There are no indications that developing countries are likely to face a crisis situation in the foreseeable future.

---

[a] This article is based on Shimizu [2014b].

However, there is a renewed awareness of the need to be prepared for risks.

This situation requires a multifaceted response from developing countries. First, they need to strengthen their liquidity support systems for emergencies, mainly by accumulating foreign currency reserves and expanding bilateral and multilateral currency swap agreements. Second, they must ensure appropriate macroeconomic policy management. Third, they need to improve their domestic financial systems.

All of these measures are used in response to increases in capital inflows, but restrictions on capital transactions also merit consideration as a way of curbing inflows. In Asia, however, efforts are focusing on the achievement of ASEAN financial integration with the establishment of the ASEAN Economic Community at the end of 2015. For this reason, the best strategy would be to accelerate regional financial integration by moving forward with the liberalization of capital transactions, while working to reduce reliance on capital from advanced countries and build robust markets.

In this chapter we will examine the current state of financial systems in ASEAN countries and analyze some of the challenges that confront them as they move toward regional integration. Section 9.2 provides a detailed analysis of the content of regional financial integration in ASEAN. Section 9.3 looks first at the strategies needed to achieve regional financial integration. This is followed by an examination of the situation in the banking sector, stock markets and bond markets, and the outlook for integration in each of these areas, as well as some of the issues that exist at present. Lastly, the conclusion shows some important approaches to regional financial integration.

9.2   Moves toward ASEAN Financial Integration

9.2.1   *Motivation for regional financial integration: The overview depicted in the AEC Blueprint*

We will look next at ASEAN financial integration, which is being pursued as part of the AEC (ASEAN Economic Community) Blueprint.

ASEAN adopted the AEC Blueprint as its roadmap for regional integration in November 2007, when the 13th ASEAN Summit was held in Singapore [ASEAN, 2008].

Although there has been significant progress toward the improvement of financial and capital markets in ASEAN, the markets are still relatively small and vulnerable to external shocks. This is reflected in the existence of restrictions on capital transactions, which have been an obstacle to regional financial integration. That is why progress toward regional financial integration has been slow compared with economic integration (Figure 9.1). The integration of labor, goods and money is commonly linked together, but there are particular problems in the area of money, including the difficulty of differentiating capital flows, and the risk of capital outflows. The development of policies to allow regional financial integration will therefore involve considerable effort.

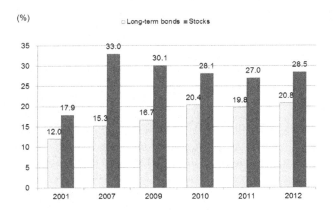

Figure 9.1. Intraregional investment ratios of Asian countries.

Notes: Investment sources: Hong Kong, Indonesia, South Korea, Malaysia, the Philippines, Singapore, and Thailand.

Investment recipients: The above countries plus China and Vietnam.

Source: IMF, *Coordinated Portfolio Investment Survey* (http://cpis.imf.org/).

The basic plan for ASEAN financial integration calls for the integration of all ASEAN financial and capital markets through the liberalization of domestic financial services and capital transactions, and the harmonization of regulations. In other words, ASEAN aims to achieve integration through liberalization and harmonization. Financial and capital markets in individual ASEAN countries are small, and this approach will allow them to achieve economies of scale. In addition, competition among markets within the region will help to strengthen financial systems and financial institutions. This will in turn improve the efficiency with which funds are allocated and ensure that appropriate financial services are available for a wide range of domestic and cross-border economic activities. With these achievements, the aim of regional financial integration is to reduce dependence on external capital and financial systems and to allocate regional savings to regional investment.

However, the achievement of financial integration in Europe has taken over 50 years, and basically there appears to be no reason why Asia should approach the process in a hasty and slipshod way. Because of the variation in the economic and financial development stages of Asian countries, ASEAN's position is that priority must be given to national sovereignty and preparations to deal with the risks that will result from integration, and that variation in the pace of integration in different countries is acceptable, especially between the original five members and Brunei, Cambodia, Laos, Myanmar, and Vietnam (BCLMV).

Financial systems in ASEAN countries are generally small, and the level of development varies from country to country. Approaches to regional financial integration will need to take these characteristics into account.

The ASEAN financial integration initiative is based on the Roadmap for Monetary and Financial Integration (RIA-Fin), which was endorsed at the 2003 ASEAN Finance Ministers Meeting. The plan outlined in the AEC Blueprint on this basis is described below. These items have been identified as steps required for the creation of a single market and production base. The goal is to create an integrated regional financial system capable of functioning efficiently.

First, financial services liberalization (FSL) will be achieved after the development and stabilization of the financial sector. Countries can liberalize as soon as their preparations are complete, and the liberalization process will be based on respect for each country's policy goals and level of economic and financial development. The specific action required is the achievement of some degree of liberalization by 2015. The ultimate target year is 2020, by which time countries should have achieved large-scale deregulation regarding all of their financial service sectors. This process is to be based on a liberalization plan consisting of a list of "pre-agreed flexibilities." The lists that make up the plan have been compiled in stages covering the periods to 2015, to 2020, and from 2020 onwards. This means that full liberalization may not be achieved by 2020. Moreover, the definition of "full liberalization" is not entirely clear.

Second, the following targets have been set concerning capital market development and integration (CMD) in the period to 2015: (1) facilitation of harmonization of rules concerning bond issuance, information disclosure and sales of securities, (2) mutual recognition of qualifications, education and experience of market professionals, (3) increased flexibility with regard to language use and enabling laws for securities issuance, (4) reassessment of withholding tax systems relating to bonds, and (5) market efforts toward the linkage of securities exchanges and bond markets, including cross-border issuance. It is not entirely clear what steps need to be carried out before these goals can be deemed to have been achieved.

Third, as with financial services liberalization, ASEAN will proceed cautiously with capital account liberalization (CAL). The plan emphasizes the need to avoid the risks of liberalization while ensuring that all member countries share the benefits. The plan calls specifically for liberalization in areas that will help to promote direct investment and capital market development. However, progress under the plan is likely to be extremely gradual, since the goal for all items is to "progressively liberalize, where appropriate and possible."

The ASEAN Secretariat is monitoring progress toward financial integration using a scorecard system. It has also commissioned the Economic Research Institute for ASEAN and East Asia (ERIA) to assess the plan. According to ERIA, the key components of financial integration should be implemented from 2015 onwards [Wihardja, 2013]. However, the establishment of the AEC at the end of 2015 is certain to provide a strong impetus for progress toward financial integration.

9.2.2 *Financial services liberalization*

In April 2011, the central bank governors of ASEAN countries formulated the ASEAN Financial Integration Framework (AFIF). This framework provides an overall picture of ASEAN's approach to financial liberalization and integration as it works toward the establishment of the AEC. The aim is to create a semi-integrated financial and capital markets by 2020.

Financial services liberalization will allow banks, insurance companies and investment companies in ASEAN countries to provide services in other countries of the region. The aim is to create an environment in which Qualified ASEAN Banks (QABs) that have reached a certain standard in terms of competitiveness and other factors will be treated on an equal footing with local banks. The ASEAN Banking Integration Framework (ABIF) was created, together with the AFIF (see above), as a structure within which QABs can be recognized.

The Asian Development Bank [2013] explains financial services liberalization in terms of three elements. First, the QAB framework will allow banks from ASEAN countries to operate in other countries in the region. To eliminate the concerns of host countries, QABs will be required to meet rigorous standards of soundness. Not many banks in the region will be able to qualify under these standards, which will function both as targets toward which banks in ASEAN countries should aspire, and also as guidelines for the establishment of prudential regulations by the banking authorities.

Second, it will be necessary to treat banks moving into markets on an equal footing with local banks. Third, to ensure the proper functioning of this framework, it will be necessary to move toward the harmonization of banking regulations in member countries. It will also be necessary to develop financial infrastructure in each country, including rating agencies, credit guarantee facilities and interbank markets. Capacity building will be a priority for countries that have not yet developed this infrastructure, and those countries will not be able to accept QABs until after this has been achieved. This means that the framework cannot be applied at the same time in every country. Moreover, the more advanced countries within the region will need to provide less developed countries with assistance on financial technology.

Progress toward regional banking integration (defined here as the expansion of banks from ASEAN members into other countries within the region) will enhance the efficiency with which funds are allocated. It will also strengthen the region's banks, facilitate the development of closer cooperative relationships, and contribute to financial sector stability. However, the facilitation of banking integration will also heighten the systemic risk by deteriorating financial performance of foreign banks operating in ASEAN countries due to their lack of understanding about the local market characteristics in the host country. Other dangers that have been highlighted include increased volatility in capital flows due to speculative cross-border transactions, and dominance of host countries' markets by foreign banks. That is why the harmonization of prudential regulations and the creation of international crisis response systems are so important. Phased liberalization is needed because of the different amounts of time required to strengthen the banking sector in each country.

ASEAN members are negotiating over details of financial services liberalization through the Working Committee on Financial Services Liberalization. Stage 6 of these negotiations has been completed, and the Committee has now entered Stage 7. As far as can be gauged from the progress of these negotiations, ASEAN is moving forward steadily with the liberalization of financial services, including insurance sector.

9.2.3 *Capital account liberalization*

The regulations that currently govern capital transactions in ASEAN countries can be summed up as follows. First, while some countries, such as Singapore, Cambodia and Indonesia, already have extremely open systems, other ASEAN members still maintain a certain level of regulation. Second, most of these regulations target capital outflows rather than inflows. This situation will need to be reconsidered from the perspective of facilitating regional integration, since it has the potential to limit capital flows among ASEAN countries while facilitating inflows of funds from outside of the region. Third, while most ASEAN members are covered by IMF Article VIII, they still impose restrictions on current account transactions. Fourth, most ASEAN countries restrict the use of their currencies overseas. Fifth, there are few restrictions on inward investment in securities, but there are numerous restrictions on overseas borrowings, and overseas lending denominated in domestic currencies. Sixth, many ASEAN countries restrict foreign exchange risk hedging by investors. Seventh, some ASEAN countries still levy withholding tax on securities investment.

Progress toward the expansion of investment, trade and business within the ASEAN region is dependent on the liberalization of capital transactions. ASEAN members have completed the task of checking and assessing their restrictions on capital transactions and are now in the process of developing liberalization roadmaps. The Working Committee on Capital Account Liberalization (WC-CAL) has stepped up its monitoring of progress toward liberalization in ASEAN countries and is also discussing policies relating to the risks of liberalization.

9.2.4   *Development of settlement systems*

The Asian Development Bank [2013] contains recommendations relating to trade settlements, money remittances, retail payments and capital market settlements. The goals identified are (1) the improvement of settlement infrastructure, (2) the standardization of settlement systems (settlement technology, market practices, regulations, etc.) to allow efficient cross-border settlements, and (3) studies concerning the linkage of settlement systems within ASEAN. Harmonized settlement systems are likely to play an important role in the AEC, and the Working Committee on Payment and Settlement Systems (WC-PSS) is assessing the current situation and making policy recommendations concerning settlement systems.

The level of settlement systems also varies according to the level of financial systems development. ASEAN countries first need to improve their domestic settlement systems, and then form links with other countries in the region.

Among the medium-term goals recommended concerning trade settlements are the facilitation of overnight (T+1) settlements of cross-border payments, and settlements in local currencies. Recommendations concerning retail payments include the diversification of the products available (e.g., ATM cards, debit cards, credit cards) and the expansion of services, such as overseas remittances. In relation to capital market settlements, the Asian Development Bank recommends the adoption of international standards for straight-through processing for both domestic and cross-border settlements, and the expansion of DVP/PVP settlements.

In a related move, the ASEAN+3 countries are working to create a settlement system to support cross-border bond transactions under the Asian Bond Markets Initiative (ABMI). Recent progress includes the completion of a reassessment of business feasibility relating to the establishment of a regional settlement intermediary (RSI) by Task Force 4. In addition, discussions are continuing within the newly established Cross-border Settlement Infrastructure Forum, which is based on voluntary participation by member countries. Inui [2014] describes the current status of settlement systems covering 10 ASEAN countries and regions, based on work carried out in the ASEAN+3 Bond Market Forum (ABMF), which is part of the ABMI. According to this paper, bond settlements are processed by central securities depositories (CSDs) operated by central banks or securities exchanges in each country. Settlements of funds are processed using real time gross settlement (RTGS) systems provided by central banks, and in many cases settlements are carried out on a delivery versus payment (DVP) basis, which means that bonds and funds are settled at the same time.

Cross-border settlements are also processed through settlement systems in individual countries. However, there are issues in areas other than settlement systems, including restrictions on capital transactions, and regulations requiring the qualification of foreign investors. Another problem is the fact that many of the elements that make up settlement systems in individual countries, such as messages and securities numbers, do not comply with international standards.

As previously noted, the priorities now are the standardization of settlement systems in individual countries, and the introduction of STP for cross-border bond transactions and settlements. Progress in these areas would reduce settlement costs and settlement risks. The key question in this context is how cross-border settlements of funds (direct settlements among the currencies of member countries) can be enabled.

The Cross-Border Settlement Infrastructure Forum, which also works collaboratively with the ABMF, has issued a report stating that the most promising regional settlement infrastructure model is not the Asian ICSD or CSD linkage model (settlements of funds using money from commercial banks), which had been considered until now, but rather a CSD-RTGS linkage model based on the linkage of CSDs and central bank fund settlement systems (RTGS) in each country.

9.2.5 *Capital market development and integration*

A key goal in the context of ASEAN's capital market liberalization efforts is capital market integration, which would allow regional issuers to implement issues in any ASEAN country, and regional investors to invest in any country in the region. Another goal is to allow intermediaries to offer their services in any country within the region, subject to approval by the authorities in their home country.

In 2009, the Implementation Plan for ASEAN Capital Markets Integration was adopted. This plan defines specific measures to compensate for the inadequate scale of capital markets in individual ASEAN countries, including the harmonization of market infrastructure with the aim of expanding intraregional cross-border transactions in securities exchanges within the ASEAN region. The main themes of the plan are the creation of an enabling environment (a framework for harmonization and mutual recognition), the creation of market infrastructure (an alliance of ASEAN securities exchanges and a governance structure, the development of new products, the strengthening of bond markets), and the strengthening of the integration process (the alignment of domestic capital market development plans, the reinforcement of organizations within ASEAN). Progress on this plan is being driven by the ASEAN Capital Markets Forum (ACMF), which was established in 2004 as a forum for discussion among securities regulatory authorities about capital market development within the ASEAN region.

As listed below, many concrete achievements have resulted from the work of the ACMF.

(a) Expedited Review Framework for Secondary Listings. A mechanism designed to reduce costs and improve efficiency for secondary listings by regional corporations within the securities exchanges of ASEAN countries by simplifying assessing procedure.

(b) ASEAN Corporate Governance Scorecard. Used to assess the corporate governance of listed companies in the ASEAN region.

(c) ASEAN Disclosure Standards. A uniform disclosure standards developed to improve the efficiency of cross-border securities issues.

(d) Work relating to the ASEAN Exchanges, which enabled trading in 210 representative stocks via an electronic network linking seven ASEAN exchanges (Indonesia, Malaysia, the Philippines, Singapore, Thailand, Hanoi, Ho Chi Minh). The establishment of this structure is being studied by subworking groups responsible for the four areas of business planning, regulation, market management and technology.

(e) Cross-Recognition of Qualification on Education and Experience of Market Professionals.

(f) ASEAN Framework for Cross-Border Offerings of Collective Investment Schemes. Known as the "fund passport" system.

(g) Development of ASEAN stock indices. In 2005, The FTSE ASEAN 180 Index and the FTSE ASEAN 40 Index were developed in collaboration with the FTSE Group of the United Kingdom.

Progress on all of these items has been led by the securities authorities of Malaysia, Singapore and Thailand. When viewed in relation to the Implementation Plan for ASEAN Capital Markets Integration, these items appear to align with the key initiatives relating to (1) a framework for harmonization and mutual recognition, or (2) an alliance of ASEAN securities exchanges and a governance structure. Items (a) through (c) relate to issues, (d) and (e) to transaction infrastructure, and (f) and (g) to investment.

Obviously there are many differences in the capital market regulations and systems and market infrastructure of ASEAN countries, and it will not be easy to overcome these differences and achieve mutual recognition. Of particular importance are tasks relating to the facilitation of cross-border securities issues, including the harmonization of disclosure standards, definition of securities and rating systems.

Work carried out by the Working Committee on Capital Market Development (WC-CMD) includes (1) the creation of the Bond Market Development Scorecard, (2) the development of a capacity building program to rectify problems identified using the scorecard, and (3) research on market development issues and policy recommendations to ASEAN members in collaboration with the ACMF. In addition, the ACMF, WC-CAL, WC-CMD and WC-PSS are continuing their efforts to improve capital market infrastructure.

9.2.6 *Other activities*

Financial integration in ASEAN involves several other processes in addition to the four items outlined above. First, there is the reinforcement of regional surveillance. Organizations monitoring economic and financial conditions in the region include the ASEAN+3 Macroeconomic Research Office (AMRO), which was established by the ASEAN+3 countries. The surveillance and capacity building programs were further strengthened with the creation of the ASEAN Integration Monitoring Office (AIMO) within the ASEAN Secretariat in May 2010.

Second, ASEAN is working to strengthen infrastructure finance. The ASEAN Infrastructure Fund (AIF)[b] was established in 2012 with the aim of strengthening physical connectivity within the region and reducing infrastructure gaps. The first project using the AIF was carried out in Indonesia in 2013, followed by projects in Indonesia, Laos and Vietnam in 2014.

---

[b] The AIF was established in Malaysia with contributions of US$335 million from ASEAN members and US$150 million from the ADB. Each year it provides loans up to a ceiling of US$75 million each for around six projects. Loans are available for projects that contribute to poverty reduction, trade expansion and the promotion of investment. The ADB manages the AIF and provides commitments for additional project co-financing.

Third, there are initiatives relating to financial inclusion and literacy. Financial literacy initiatives are led by Brunei, which has established a forum for information sharing and other activities. ASEAN countries are also cooperating on financial inclusion initiatives.

9.3 Financial Systems in ASEAN Countries

9.3.1 *Overview of financial systems and strategies for regional integration*

As discussed in the previous section, the ASEAN countries need to move toward regional financial integration while also reducing the risk of financial crises by responding appropriately to expanding flows of foreign investment. A key priority in this context is the reinforcement of financial and capital markets and financial institutions in individual ASEAN countries. In this section, we will examine financial systems in ASEAN countries from this perspective.

There is considerable variation in the level of development of financial systems in ASEAN countries. Even where the level of development is similar, there are differences in other characteristics, such as market size and financial infrastructure and regulations. For this reason, individual countries have different needs in relation to financial integration, and while some countries want regional integration, others regard links with outside of the region as more important.

This means that regional integration will need to be open rather than closed. Moreover, since integration will also cause competition to intensify, it will be necessary to strengthen the competitiveness of financial systems in individual countries, and to reduce development gaps between countries. ASEAN countries need to debate their approach to regional financial integration fully and will need to move forward gradually, while remaining focused on the 2015 and 2020 deadlines.

A comparison of financial assets as percentages of GDP shows that while Malaysia, Singapore and Thailand rank alongside the EU countries, the ratios for Vietnam, the Philippines and Indonesia are similar to those for developing countries with similar income levels (Table 9.1). The ratios for Brunei, Cambodia, Laos and Myanmar are extremely low, and their stock and bond markets are underdeveloped. Financial inclusion varies widely within the ASEAN region. There is also considerable disparity in the insurance sector, and the urgent need for improvement is apparent from the fact that the average number of people served by each life insurance company branch is over 300,000.

Table 9.1. Financial and capital markets as percentages of GDP.

	2000				2012			
	Banks (domestic credit)	Bond market issue balance	Stock market capital-ization	Total	Banks (domestic credit)	Bond Market issue balance	Stock market capital-ization	Total
China	112.3	16.9	48.5	177.7	157.1	46.3	44.9	248.4
Hong Kong	133.8	35.2	363.1	532.2	201.3	67.6	1,078.3	1,347.1:
Indonesia	52.8	32.0	16.2	101.1	39.4	12.7	48.8	100.9
Japan	227.8	96.2	66.7	390.8	230.5	196.3	58.6	485.4
South Korea	102.5	66.6	27.8	196.9	178.5	130.2	104.4	413.2
Malaysia	138.4	73.2	120.7	332.3	135.3	107.3	153.1	395.7
Philippines	34.9	25.9	31.2	92.0	52.4	39.6	91.7	183.7
Singapore	87.1	47.2	164.5	298.8	99.0	81.2	269.1	449.3
Thailand	110.0	25.3	23.8	159.1	131.5	76.1	106.5	314.1

Source: Asian Bond Monitor and, *World Economic Outlook Database.*

Financial systems in ASEAN countries are dominated by banks, although Malaysia and Singapore are starting to improve their capital markets. However, the small size of the ASEAN economies is reflected in their financial and capital markets, which are small by world standards, and it will not be easy to improve their international competitiveness and increase their presence. Moreover, even though stock markets are expanding in step with economic development, the low level of liquidity means that markets are vulnerable to fluctuations in the activities of foreign investors. These factors are all incentives for capital market integration. Namely, the realization of economies of scale is an important reason for integration. However, this goal can only be achieved if each country has robust domestic markets.

Moreover, while the achievement of financial integration in some form will bring benefits, it will also create risks different from those encountered in the past. This is an important issue requiring countermeasures at the regional level.

When diverse financial systems are integrated, there is no way to ensure that all participants will benefit, and inevitably some will be disadvantaged. Considering this point, a number of priorities will need to be tackled as ASEAN moves toward financial integration. First, it will be necessary to engage in continual debate about ways to reconcile differences in the needs of individual member countries. Second, ASEAN will need to work to reduce differences in development levels, which are partially responsible for differences in the needs of each country. Third, in addition to efforts to enhance the competitiveness of financial and capital markets and financial institutions in member countries, it will also be necessary to improve institutional infrastructure, such as financial regulations. In this context, the development of the banking sector will be a particular priority in the BCLMV countries, which are still in the early stages of financial development. Fourth, the specifics of integration and the ways that integration benefits national interests must be acceptable to member countries. Fifth, there should be a schedule for the achievement of integration. Sixth, regional institutions should be created to deal with the risks associated with integration. Seventh, financial authorities should provide leadership for the steady implementation of integration plans.

The most important priority at present appears to be the improvement of financial systems in member countries. Efforts to raise the level of these systems will enhance the feasibility of ASEAN financial integration. Also, the development of robust financial systems will lead to the creation of structures capable of coping with inflows of capital from outside of the region.

ASEAN is moving toward financial integration not only because of the progress toward integration at the real economic level, but also because of a loss of confidence in capital from outside of the region, which has repeatedly flowed into and out of the region since the Asian financial crisis. After experiencing the crisis, however, Asian countries have dramatically improved their emergency liquidity support systems, in part by accumulating foreign currency reserves. As a result, they were able to respond appropriately to the sudden decline in liquidity resulting from the 2008 Lehman shock. Efforts to improve financial systems are steadily producing benefits, including the recovery of financial soundness in the banking sector, and the establishment of a position for Asian bonds as a target for investment by investors in advanced countries. These achievements can be seen as evidence of a measurable strengthening of the capacity of ASEAN countries to accommodate capital inflows from outside of the region.

ASEAN countries have a voracious demand for funds, especially for infrastructure development, and will inevitably continue to rely on funds from outside of the region to some extent. The most important priority for ASEAN in this context is to combine the pursuit of financial integration with continuing efforts to strengthen financial systems to ensure that the region can achieve a form of integration that will allow it to remain open and outward-looking.

9.3.2   *The banking sector*

The state of the banking sector

The following analysis examines the financial systems of ASEAN countries by looking first at the banking sector, and then at stock markets and bond markets. We can identify a number of characteristics in the banking sectors of ASEAN countries[c]. First, banking reforms implemented since the Asian financial crisis have dramatically improved banks' financial soundness and earning performance, with the result that banks in ASEAN now compare favorably with banks in advanced countries on this point. Second, because banks had maintained sound management policies, they were affected little by the global financial crisis. In fact, their financial positions have tended to improve continuously since the crisis. Third, there has been no significant change

---

[c] For a detailed examination of the banking sectors of Malaysia, Thailand, Indonesia, and Vietnam, see Japan Research Institute Limited [2012].

in the relative size and importance of the banking sector within domestic financial systems. ASEAN countries still have financial systems centering on banks, which were seen as a major cause of the Asian financial crisis. Fourth, the size of banks is relatively small by international standards. For example, banks in ASEAN countries are between one-fiftieth and one-hundredth the size of Japanese megabanks. Fifth, there is a major gap between ASEAN and advanced countries in terms of financial inclusion, including the number of bank branches and bank deposit accounts per unit of population. Sixth, there is considerable variation among ASEAN countries in terms of levels of banking sector development, bank size, and financial inclusion. This situation will be a major impediment to progress toward regional financial integration[d].

An analysis of progress toward regional banking integration in this environment shows that while some banks from Singapore, Malaysia, and Thailand (usually the top 1–3 banks in each country) have expanded into a number countries in the region, their overseas activities are less extensive than those of major Western Banks, such as Standard Chartered, Citibank, and HSBC (Table 9.2). Moreover, the majority of ASEAN banks are reluctant to expand into other countries within the region, mainly because of the small scale of their operations and their lack of international competitiveness. Another possible reason is the fact that the domestic financial markets in ASEAN have not yet been fully developed and still offer ample scope for growth.

---

[d] In relation to this issue, a senior official of the Philippine central bank commented in February 2014 that the small size of Philippine banks meant that the Philippines was unlikely to benefit from integration in the present environment, and that banks needed to prepare for integration by strengthening their positions in their home markets and improving their risk management systems.

Table 9.2. Presence of banks in ASEAN countries (End of 2011).

		Brunei	Cambodia	Indonesia	Laos	Malaysia	Myanmar	Philippines	Singapore	Thailand	Vietnam
Global	HSBC	o		o		o		o	o	o	o
	Standard Chartered	o	Rep	o	Rep	o	Rep	o	o	o	o
	Citibank	o		o		o		o	o	o	o
Japan	SMBC		Rep	o		o	Rep	Rep	o	o	o
	Mizuho FG			o		o		o	o	o	o
	Bank of Tokyo-Mitsubishi UFJ		o	o		o		o	o	o	o
Indonesia	Mandiri			o					o		
	BCA			o							
	BNI			o					o		
Malaysia	Maybank	o	o	o		o	Rep	o	o	o	o
	Public Bank		o			o	Rep				o
	CIMB	o	o	o	o	o	Rep		o	o	o
Philippines	Metrobank							o	Rep		
	BDO							o			
	BPI							o			
Singapore	DBS	o Off Shore/ Rep		o		o	Rep	Rep	o	Rep	Rep
	UOB			o		o	Rep	o	o	o	o
	OCBC			o		o	Rep		o	o	o
Thailand	SCB		o		o				o	o	o
	Bangkok Bank			o	o	o	Rep	o	o	o	JV
	B. Ayudhya				o					o	

Note: Rep=Representative office
Source: Asian Development Bank [2014:148–149].

ASEAN countries also seek to protect their local banks by restricting participation by foreign banks and discriminating against foreign banks in their domestic markets. Restrictions of these types were substantially relaxed after the Asian financial crisis so that foreign capital could be used to drive the bank restructuring and rehabilitation process that followed the crisis. However, there has since been a resurgence of moves to protect and strengthen local banks by limiting participation by foreign banks. In 2012, for example, Indonesia lowered the ceiling for foreign ownership from 99% to 40%. On the other hand, in July 2014, the Philippines announced that it intended to abolish the 60% ceiling on foreign ownership, and Myanmar has finally started to issue business licenses to foreign banks. These examples show how differences in the development stages, financial and capital market development needs and stances of ASEAN countries are reflected in restrictions on participation by foreign banks.

The insurance sector is relatively open to foreign participation, but local insurance companies lack competitiveness, and there have been few cases of overseas expansion. Most of the companies that have gained shares of ASEAN markets are insurance companies from advanced countries, and there has been little progress toward integration within the region.

Outlook for bank integration, priorities for the banking sector

Most of the foreign banks that have established operations in ASEAN countries are from outside of the region. While this situation has started to change, the limited scale of local banks means that only a minority of banks are likely to achieve QAB status in the immediate future, and that progress toward integration will therefore be gradual. There is little possibility of comprehensive banking integration as seen in the EU.

However, Asian financial systems center on banks, and bank integration is likely to play a central role in financial integration. The ASEAN Senior Level Committee on Financial Integration (SLC) was formed as a high-level organization for the planning and monitoring of financial integration.

The four core components of the ASEAN Banking Integration Framework (ABIF) are (1) harmonization of principles of prudential regulations, (2) the creation of the infrastructure required for financial stability (macroprudential policies, crisis management policies, deposit insurance, etc.), (3) the provision of capacity building programs for the BCLMV countries, and (4) the adoption of standards for QABs. Working groups have been formed with responsibility for each of these areas. To minimize the risks associated with integration, it will also be necessary to establish regional-level monitoring and supervisory functions. In addition to the development of closer cooperation among authorities within the region, AMRO and the Chiang Mai Initiative Multilateralization (CMIM), which have been established within the ASEAN+3 framework, are also expected to play a significant role in this area.

Despite extensive debate by the four working groups, the positions of individual ASEAN members still differ. Malaysia, which has a small domestic market but a highly developed financial system, would benefit considerably from integration and is actively promoting the ABIF. Indonesia, on the other hand, has a large domestic market, but the competitiveness of its financial institutions appears to be relatively weak, and there is ongoing debate about the relative merits and costs of integration.

Differences in the size of financial markets and development levels of ASEAN members are also reflected in significant variation in the level of prudential regulations and infrastructure supporting financial stability. The original ASEAN members and the BCLMV countries will need to follow a double-track approach that gives priority to capacity building in the latter group. However, it will not be easy to create a roadmap based on this method that will ultimately lead to the integration of the entire region, and there is a strong possibility that funds will be concentrated in particular countries during the integration process.

As is apparent from the preceding analysis, there are still many issues affecting the bank integration process. While it would be possible for banks that are relatively competitive within the region to lead the way in adapting to integration, it will not be possible to achieve integration on a level that will bring real benefits without consideration for those that cannot keep up with competition.

The priorities for the banking sector are summed up in Figure 9.2. First, it will be necessary to improve banking services in ways that contribute to economic development, including the promotion of financial inclusion, and an involvement in domestic demand-related business areas. Second, the competitiveness of banks will need to be strengthened. There are many possible strategies to achieve this, including the facilitation of mergers, the improvement of operating efficiency, human resource development, and the development of new business areas. However, banks must also maintain their present level of soundness by avoiding excessive expansion of their activities. Third, to maintain soundness during the integration process, it will be necessary to develop and harmonize banking regulatory and supervisory systems. Fourth, support for BCLMV countries in the area of financial technology will need to be stepped up in order to reduce disparity among ASEAN members.

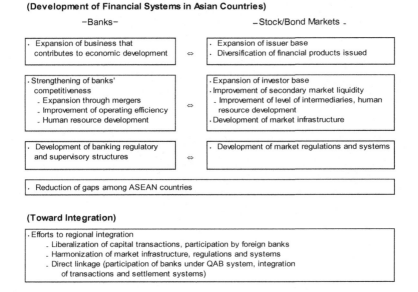

Figure 9.2. Priorities for the development of financial systems in Asia.
Source: Compiled by the author.

9.3.3 *Stock markets*

The State of Stock Markets[e]

ASEAN stock markets have achieved rapid growth over the past 10 years. The markets can be broadly divided into four groups. The first group consists of one market in a financial hub (Singapore). Singapore is a financial hub for the whole of Asia, including ASEAN, and in addition to its wide range of financial products and market participants, it also has a large offshore market. Established domestic markets (Malaysia and Thailand) form the second group. These markets have ample domestic issuer and investor bases, and Islamic financial products are a feature of the Malaysian market. The level of over-the-counter trading in financial derivatives is still low in both of these markets. Investment from overseas is affected by certain limitations, including restrictions on capital transactions. The third group consists of still developing domestic markets (Indonesia, the Philippines). While these markets have expanded rapidly, the size of domestic issuer and investor bases is limited. Institutional investors are still at the developing stage. The underdeveloped markets of the BCLMV countries make up the fourth group. These markets are at the initial stage of development, and financial infrastructure and regulatory frameworks are still being developed. The domestic investor base is small, and apart from Brunei and Cambodia, all countries in this group tightly regulate capital transactions.

A variety of capital market reforms have been implemented by ASEAN countries. The Singapore exchange was established in 1999, while the Philippine Stock Exchange became a joint stock corporation in 2001 and was listed in 2003. In Indonesia, the Jakarta and Surabaya Stock Exchanges merged in 2007. Malaysia has gradually eased restrictions on capital transactions, and investment in domestic securities by non-residents has expanded. Thailand announced capital market development plans in 2002 and 2006.

---

[e] See Oliver Wyman and CIMB ASEAN Research Institute [2013] and Korea Institute of Finance [2014] for analyses of stock markets.

Over the past 10 years, the number of listed companies in all ASEAN countries has increased by 30%. In Indonesia and Malaysia in particular, the trend toward corporate privatization is helping to drive this growth. In the past stock market intermediaries were mostly global banks from advanced countries. More recently, however, bank-affiliated securities companies in Malaysia and Singapore have adopted strategies that are clearly designed to promote regional market integration, and they are playing an increasingly important role in the region. In addition, institutional investors, such as pension funds and insurance companies, are expanding in ASEAN countries in response to a conspicuous build-up of savings, improvements in healthcare and pension systems, and other factors. At the same time, there has been an easing of restrictions on investment. There has also been a rapid increase in foreign investment in stocks and government bonds.

Outlook for stock market integration, priorities for stock markets

As we have already seen, the main reason for economic and financial integration in ASEAN is the small size of individual countries regarding economies and financial and capital markets. As the economic growth of China and India began to accelerate in the 2000s, the ASEAN countries realized with alarm that their stock markets would be unable to compete with other markets without further improvements in a number of areas, including secondary market liquidity, transaction costs, product line-ups, and financial technology innovation. This provided the motive to speed up regional integration, which had still not reached a satisfactory level, leading in 2009 to the announcement of the Implementation Plan for ASEAN Capital Markets Integration.

Regional integration would result in improved international competitiveness resulting from the expansion of the investor base and product lineups, the reinforcement of domestic markets, and the improvement of liquidity. ASEAN would be recognized as a single asset class, and the interest of foreign investors could be expected to rise. These changes would in turn lead to accelerated economic growth and the diversification of channels for procuring and investing funds.

Integration would also be expected to bring benefits for market participants. First, the potential benefits for investors include better financial products and services, lower transaction costs thanks to competition among intermediaries, and the diversification of investment targets. Second, lower service provision costs, made possible by economies of scale and scope, and an expanded investor base are among the likely benefits for intermediaries. Third, issuers would benefit from lower securities issuance costs thanks to the harmonization of regulations and other systems. Fourth, regulatory authorities would benefit from the development of appropriate regulations for cross-border transactions as the integration process advances.

Stock market integration is likely to be strengthened through harmonization and mutual recognition, and through the role of the ASEAN exchanges, which are expected to support integration as market infrastructure. Other key factors will include the development of products that will facilitate cross-border transactions, such as cross-border sales frameworks for collective investment schemes.

Progress toward integration can also be expected to accelerate the development of markets in relatively less developed countries. However, care will be needed to ensure that regional integration does not hinder the market development efforts of individual countries. This is another reason why policy adjustment efforts and the establishment of clearly defined short-, medium- and long-term targets are essential.

The needs of ASEAN members differ according to their specific circumstances, and differences in development levels will also be an issue in relation to stock market integration. There is also variation in legal and regulatory systems. For these reasons, ASEAN should aim for gradual integration through the expansion of cross-border transactions rather than through the creation of a single market. It will also be necessary to take an opt-in approach that allows countries to participate when they are able. The integration process is unlikely to move forward unless each country is confident that they will be able to benefit from integration.

There are several priorities relating to stock markets. First, it will be necessary to expand the investor base. Stock investment is not widespread, so there are few individual investors. Only 9% of

Singaporeans invest in stocks, compared with 35% in Hong Kong and 17% in Australia. Individual investors account for 60% of transactions on the South Korean stock exchange, compared with just 20% in Malaysia. The scale of institutional investors is also small in ASEAN countries other than Malaysia and Singapore, and their investment strategies tend to be conservative.

Second, while ASEAN stock markets have achieved a certain level of development, as evidenced by ratios of market capitalization to GDP and other indicators, most are also affected by the problem of low liquidity, which is a source of market instability. One possible solution for this problem would be the expansion of the individual investor base, but more wide-ranging measures should also be considered.

Third, the level of cross-border investment within the ASEAN region remains low (Table 9.3). ASEAN members will therefore need to implement a wide range of measures, such as the harmonization of market infrastructure, to expand cross-border investment. Another approach that could be effective would be to educate individual investors about the potential of regional companies as attractive targets for investment.

Table 9.3. Balance of cross-border stock investment in ASEAN (2010).

Recipient country	Source Country							
	Indonesia	Malaysia	Philippines	Singapore	Thailand	Total	Investment from the world	Investment from ASEAN (%)
Indonesia	...	766	...	2,877	21	3,664	60,971	6.0
Malaysia	...	...	...	8,613	12	8,625	55,467	15.6
Philippines	...	28	...	974	2	1,004	17,089	5.9
Singapore	22	7,196	5	...	585	7,808	132,728	5.9
Thailand	...	320	...	2,978	...	3,298	55,443	5.9
Vietnam	...	31	...	395	12	438	2,698	16.2
Total	22	8,341	5	15,837	631	24,836	324,395	7.7
Investment	948	25,050	19	194,121	5,035	225,173	15,503,684	1.5
Investment to ASEAN (%)	2.3	33.3	24.6	8.2	12.5	11.0	2.1	

Note 1: China and Vietnam are not included among the source countries due to the non-availability of data.
Note 2: The figure 15,503,684 at the lower right represents total world stock investment balance.
Source: IMF, *Coordinated Portfolio Investment Survey* (http://cpis.imf.org).

As outlined earlier in this article, Malaysia, Singapore and Thailand are leading progress toward stock market integration. The smooth transition toward integration among these three countries is significant as a successful model for other ASEAN countries to follow. However, there is a vital need for further home market development to ensure that these other countries can really participate. What is needed specifically is further improvement, liberalization and harmonization in such areas as capital transaction regulations, tax systems, capital market regulations, product lineups, and corporate governance.

Fourth, human resource development is a vital priority. There is a shortage of capital market experts in ASEAN countries, and in addition to the development of market infrastructure and regulatory frameworks, the recruitment and training of these specialists will also be extremely important.

9.3.4 *Bond markets*

The state of bond markets

Excessive reliance on borrowings from domestic and foreign banks because of the underdeveloped state of bond markets within the region has been seen as one of the triggers of the 1997 financial crisis. Recognition of this problem has led to bond market development efforts by governments in the region, and to regional financial cooperation through the ABMI and other forums. The following is a brief analysis of the characteristics of ASEAN bond markets[f].

First, the Asian market as a whole has expanded significantly since the financial crisis, both in absolute terms and also as a percentage of the world bond market (Table 9.4). However, the dramatic growth of the Chinese market is responsible for a large share of this expansion, and we need to discount this factor. We also need to be aware of the extremely small size of the market at the starting point.

---

[f] References with detailed discussions of Asian bond markets include Shimizu [2014a].

Table 9.4. Increase in outstanding issues in Asian bond markets (in US$ billions).

	End of 1997		End of 2013		Expansion (Times)		GDP Ratio (%)	
	Govt. bonds	Corporate bonds	Govt. bonds	Corporate bonds	Govt. bonds	Corporate bonds	Govt. bonds	Corporate bonds
China	45.1	42.7	3,073	1,652	68.1	38.7	32.7	17.6
Hong Kong	13.1	28.0	108	86	8.2	3.1	39.6	31.5
Indonesia	0.9	3.3	90	18	100.0	5.5	12.0	2.4
South Korea	32.5	120.8	626	1,015	19.3	8.4	47.9	77.6
Malaysia	19.4	37.7	182	130	9.4	3.4	60.7	43.1
Philippines	16.6	0.0	87	13	5.2	—	33.6	5.1
Singapore	13.1	10.6	150	92	11.5	8.7	51.1	31.4
Thailand	1.4	9.0	214	62	152.9	6.9	58.7	16.9
Total	142.1	252.1	4,530	3,068	31.9	12.2	—	—
Total (excl. China)	97.0	209.4	1,457	1,416	15.0	6.8	—	—

Note: GDP ratios as of the end of 2013.
Source: BIS data for figures as of the end of 1997, Asian Bonds Online for figures as of the end of 2013.

Second, as with the banking sector and stock markets, the level of market development varies widely among countries in the region. This is apparent from ratios of outstanding bond issues to GDP. Nor is the average ratio for the region particularly high. Financial systems in ASEAN countries are dominated by banks, and compared with stock markets, which have expanded to some extent, bond markets offer the greatest scope for development.

Third, while the development of the government bond and corporate bond markets is in balance to some extent, the development of the corporate bond market involves greater difficulties. The development of the government bond market is a prerequisite for that of the corporate bond market. The corporate bond issuer base is weighted toward certain types of issuers, such as financial institutions, infrastructure-related companies, government-affiliated companies and a few large corporations. Reasons for the lack of growth in corporate bond issues in the past include the stagnation of real investment by corporations, and a tendency to prefer financing from retained earnings or through share issues. In addition, Cambodia, Laos, and Myanmar have only just reached the stage at which they will need to start developing their bond markets.

Secondary market liquidity is low. Reasons for this include the fact that many institutional investors in ASEAN are still at the development stage, and the fact that the usual investment style is buy and hold. Another factor is the general lack of development of markets for hedging tools, such as derivatives and repos.

Fourth, bond market development has been approached as a policy priority. Different countries have implemented different policies, and while those policies have resulted in market development, they have not always led to the achievement of the goals adopted when the ABMI was first created, specifically the reduction of borrowing from domestic and foreign banks, and the creation of balanced financial systems.

Fifth, there has been qualitative development of bond markets, in the sense that quantitative expansion has been accompanied by creation of robust markets. Some observers have pointed out that bond markets functioned as a "spare tire" by providing those seeking funds with an alternative to international capital markets and domestic banking sectors during the Lehman shock. With the additional impetus provided by global monetary easing and the rapid growth of Asian economies, the importance of these markets as targets for investment from advanced countries has risen dramatically. However, this has also had a negative impact by heightening market instability.

Sixth, although there has been gradual progress toward regional integration, the level of integration remains low (Table 9.5). Compared with investors in advanced countries, however, Asian investors generally have a regional bias and invest a higher percentage of their assets within the region. In addition, there now appears to be a growing trend toward investment in Asian bonds among Japanese investors. This suggests that Asia, including Japan, can be expected to move further toward regional integration in the area of bond transactions in the future.

In addition, recently there has been an increase in dollar-denominated bond issues by Asian issuers, resulting in part from low interest rates in advanced countries. Many of these dollar-denominated bonds have low ratings, and some observers have warned that repayment risk could increase. Another factor contributing to the increase in issues is the fact that a variety of issuing structures are available in dollar-denominated bond markets. Asian issuers and investors are rapidly becoming more sophisticated, leading to the diversification of bond issues. One example of this pattern is the growth of covered bond issues in Singapore.

Table 9.5. Balance of cross-border bond investment in ASEAN (2010).

Recipient Country	Source Country						Investment from the world	Investment from ASEAN (%)
	Indonesia	Malaysia	Philippines	Singapore	Thailand	Total		
Indonesia	...	253	695	8,054	42	9,043	35,735	25.3
Malaysia	12	...	18	6,468	125	6,624	39,662	16.7
Philippines	...	512	...	1,687	46	2,245	25,113	8.9
Singapore	622	1,967	96	...	23	2,707	34,831	7.8
Thailand	...	165	...	2,280	...	2,445	10,186	24.0
Vietnam	...	...	...	91	...	91	2,633	3.4
Total	634	2,897	810	18,580	235	23,155	148,159	15.6
Investment to the world	4,432	10,770	5,266	126,746	13,311	160,524	21,735,503	.7
Investment to ASEAN (%)	14.3	26.9	15.4	14.7	1.8	14.4	.7	

Note 1: China and Vietnam are not included among the source countries due to the non-availability of data.
Note 2: The figure 21,735,503 at the lower right represents total world bond investment balance.
Source: IMF, *Coordinated Portfolio Investment Survey* (htttp://cpis.imf.org/).

Outlook for bond market integration, priorities for bond markets

Initiatives toward ASEAN financial integration currently appear not to include active moves to integrate bond markets. On the other hand, efforts through the ABMI have been based from the outset on the view that cross-border transactions should be facilitated. Current efforts are focusing mainly on the facilitation of issues, including cross-border issues, through the establishment of the Credit Guarantee and Investment Facility (CGIF) as a guarantee institution for corporate bond issues within the ASEAN region, the maintenance of the *Asian Bonds Online* website by the Asian Development Bank to provide information about Asian bond markets, and the efforts to standardize bond issuing rules and to improve and integrate regional settlement systems through the ABMF.

The target as far as the standardization of bond issuing rules is concerned is the establishment of the ASEAN+3 Multi-Currency Bond Issuance Framework (AMBIF) as a common regional bond issuance program for professional investors. Mutual recognition under this framework will allow greater integration of bond markets for professional investors in each member country. When it was first established, the ABMF was expected to take a top-down approach to the creation of offshore markets in Asia. However, a bottom-up approach was found to be more practical, and this now appears to be the most appropriate strategy. Even so, the achievement of mutual recognition will not be easy. The Joint Statement of the ASEAN+3 Finance Ministers and Central Bank Governors Meeting in May 2014 acknowledges the progress of efforts to "clarify commonalities and differences of bond issuance documentation and procedures," but so far this work does not appear to have resulted in any actual bond issues [ASEAN Finance Ministers' Meeting, 2014].

There are several priorities for bond markets. First, it will be necessary to expand the issuer base (Table 9.6). As with investors, one approach to this task would be to attract overseas issuers. It would also be necessary to create bond markets for companies with low credit ratings to allow bond issues by small and medium-sized enterprises.

Second, the investor base will need to be expanded. There has been some diversification of the investor base, but more needs to be done to improve secondary market liquidity. Expectations toward investors should focus on foreign as well as domestic investors. There is a risk that increased participation by foreign investors would lead to market instability. However, with their advanced investment technology and diverse investment styles, there would also be significant benefits. Foreign investment in corporate bonds could also be expected to increase.

Markets would also benefit from diversification of the investment styles of domestic investors. Pension systems should be improved, in part as a way of expanding the institutional investor base. There is also the view that what bond markets need is not more investors but more issuers, but the diversification of investor demand is likely to result in increased issues. Another way to increase investment in corporate bonds would be to ease investment restrictions for pension funds and insurance companies and the government bond holding requirements for banks.

Table 9.6. Overview of current conditions and issues in the corporate bond markets of five ASEAN countries.

	Singapore	Malaysia	Thailand	Philippines	Indonesia
Market overview, issuers, products	. The bond market has expanded rapidly since 2008. Overseas issuers have also increased their bond issues in Singapore. . Products issued are becoming more diverse, including sukuk and yuan-denominated bonds.	. There is limited scope for expansion of the government bond market, but there is room for expansion of the corporate bond market. . Indonesian and Thai issuers are issuing bonds in Malaysia. . Securitization is expected to increase.	. There is scope for further expansion of government bond issues. Corporate bonds are in short supply. There have been little issues by government-affiliated companies. . The relatively high number of issues with low ratings is a feature of the market. . Issues by foreign issuers are restricted. . Sukuk issues are expected to increase.	. Approval for issues takes considerable time. . Credit spreads do not function efficiently and are not necessarily accurate. . The number of issues is limited, and the size per issue is small.	. The level of market development is similar to that of Malaysia in the late 1990s. . Issuer diversification is needed. . Indonesia is an Islamic country, and although the Sukuk market is expected to expand, it is still small at present.
Investors	. Investors are mainly private sector banks. . There is little investment in foreign bonds by domestic investors.	. There is a "rating cliff," and investment in bonds with ratings of single A or below is minimal. . Few individuals or overseas investors participate in the corporate bond market.	. The percentage of foreign investors in government bonds is relatively high, but there is little foreign investment in corporate bonds.	. Individual investors are almost non-existent, and institutional investors are not well developed.	. There are almost no individual investors in corporate bonds.
Liquidity	. Because of the saving surplus, bonds are basically held until maturity ("buy and hold")	. Bonds with low ratings have low liquidity.	. Market liquidity is low because of the imposition of capital gains taxes on individual investors, who account for the majority of investment in the corporate bond market. . There are no functioning market makers.	. Transactions are small, and liquidity is low.	. Bond market liquidity is low, and risk premiums are large.

Source: Compiled using articles from *Asiamoney* (now known as Global Capital Asia).

Third, there should be efforts to improve market infrastructure and institutions that encompass harmonization and standardization. As noted earlier in this article, the development of settlement systems for securities and funds is especially important, and some form of standardization of the rating methods used in ASEAN countries would also be useful. Other essential steps include the development of derivatives markets, and the abolition of withholding tax.

Fourth, efforts toward market integration are needed. Like the banking sector and stock markets, however, bond markets are extremely diverse, and there is continuing debate about meaningful approaches to integration.

9.4 Conclusions

9.4.1 *Need for reconciliation of national interests and support for less developed countries*

In this final section, we will summarize the key points for regional financial integration. Regional financial integration would lead to an increase in cross-border financial and capital market transactions and would also facilitate the reciprocal use of markets in ASEAN countries. Prerequisites for this include the liberalization of capital transactions, and the harmonization and mutual recognition of regulations, systems, market infrastructure and other elements.

ASEAN financial integration would bring a variety of benefits, including economies of scale, improvements in the quantity and quality of services on offer thanks to the increased competiveness of the region's financial systems, support for member countries' economic development and integration at the real economic level, the reduction of disparities in the economies and financial systems of ASEAN countries, and increased circulation of funds in the region, leading to a reduced reliance on outside funds. Even the relatively less developed ASEAN countries would enjoy significant benefits from integration.

However, ASEAN is characterized by the generally small size of member countries' financial systems, and by wide disparities between countries in the region. Integration would be driven mainly by private sector economic entities and would lead to escalating competition, and not everyone could be a winner. As far as the integration of labor and goods is concerned, it would be possible to discover factors that would give relatively less developed countries an advantage, such as lower wages and abundant natural resources. However, there would be few such factors in relation to financial integration. This characteristic of financial transactions is responsible for the difficulty of moving forward with regional financial integration. From this perspective, it becomes clear that the reconciliation of national interests and the reduction of disparities between ASEAN countries will be important priorities. The reduction of disparities will require the reinforcement of financial technology assistance systems for the less developed countries, but this process is likely to take considerable time.

Decisions about whether competition should be encouraged or curbed will need to be made on a case-by-case basis, taking a range of factors into account. A balanced approach is needed.

9.4.2 *Contribution to economic development as a criterion for moves toward integration*

Contribution to economic development is the fundamental purpose of a financial system and should remain a focus during the integration process. Volz [2013] states that regional banking integration should contribute to regional economic development by giving priority to trade finance and infrastructure finance, and that the emergence of Asian banks as leading international banks is not an essential goal. ASEAN countries also need to be aware that there is a mutually facilitating relationship between regional economic development and financial integration. The most important priority is to discourage the excessive pursuit of profit in ways that do not contribute to the support of real economic activity, and instead to aim for the creation of sound, robust financial systems.

Specifically, the key issues for banks are the types of companies and individuals that should be given loans, and the areas of business on which to focus. The important questions in the case of equity and bond markets are the types of issuers to attract and the types of products to issue.

The overall priority is to allocate funds toward productive purposes. Infrastructure finance is especially important in the current situation.

Another key issue is the ability of financial systems to cope with demographic aging, the expansion of the middle class, environmental degradation, the increased frequency of disasters, and other changes.

9.4.3   *The need to address risks*

Because regional financial integration opens markets up to foreign participation, it also results in increased risk. The prerequisites for the liberalization of capital transactions include sound macroeconomic policy management and the improvement of domestic financial systems. The lower the level of economic and financial development, the lower is the extent to which these prerequisites are met. Integration can bring major benefits for the relatively less developed countries in the region, but these countries also face the greatest risks. The full benefits of integration cannot be realized unless the prerequisites for liberalization are met. This means that the obvious choice is an approach whereby countries participate in integration when they are ready. Full liberalization of capital transactions is not an easy goal for any country.

The creation of crisis preparedness systems also plays a vital role in reducing risks. Related measures include capital flow monitoring, the reinforcement of emergency liquidity support systems, the strengthening of financial regulations and the improvement of financial supervision. These preparations need to be made on a regional basis, which will require the harmonization of regulatory and supervisory systems. ASEAN has no central agency responsible for promoting regional integration, and the integration process is instead based on respect for each country's autonomy. Given this situation, the resolution of issues such as the harmonization of financial regulations and the establishment of regional financial supervisory organizations will be long-term challenges. ASEAN will need to maintain a balance between progress toward integration and risk management within these limitations.

Asian financial systems have not become the source of a major financial crisis since the 1997 financial crisis. As they move toward regional financial integration, the ASEAN countries will need to maintain the soundness of their financial systems.

9.4.4   *Reinforcement of financial systems the most important priority*

Reinforcement of each country's financial system will be a prerequisite for progress toward regional integration. This will involve a range of specific priorities. The priorities for banks include the improvement of operating efficiency, the development of new business areas, human resource development, and the facilitation of inter-bank mergers. Among the priorities for stock and bond markets are the expansion of issuer and investor bases, human resource development, the development of financial products, the improvement and harmonization of market infrastructure, systems and regulations, and the improvement of secondary market liquidity. The expansion of the domestic investor base is also important from the viewpoint of coping with capital flows. Growth in the number of issuers and investors who are involved in cross-border transactions can be expected to result in accelerated market expansion and development.

The reinforcement of financial systems in ASEAN countries in step with progress toward ASEAN financial integration would contribute to economic development while also helping to reduce risk. Another benefit would be the creation of structures to accommodate funds from outside of the region. This leads to the conclusion that the development of robust financial systems capable of supporting open integration is the most important goal from a long-term perspective.

References

ASEAN, (2008) ASEAN Economic Community Blueprint.
ASEAN Finance Ministers' Meeting, (2014) Joint Ministerial Statement of the 18th AFMM, Apr. 5.
Asian Development Bank, *Asia Bond Monitor* (various issues) via AsianBonds Online portal (asianbondsonline.adb.org).
Asian Development Bank, (2013) The Road to ASEAN Financial Integration.
Asian Development Bank, (2014) ASEAN 2030: Toward a Borderless Economic Community.

Inui, T. (2014), *Ajia ni okeru Kurosuboda Kessai Infura no Seibi to Kongo no Tenbo* (The Development of and Future Outlook for Cross-Border Settlement Infrastructure in Asia), Hitachi Research Institute, March.

Japan Research Institute Limited, (2012) The Roles and Functions of the Banking Sector in the Financial System of the ASEAN+3 Region, ASEAN+3 Research Group Final Report, Mar.

Korea Institute of Finance, (2014) SWOT Analysis on the Capital Market Infrastructures in the ASEAN+3 Member Countries and Its Implications, ASEAN+3 Research Group Final Report, Feb.

Oliver Wyman and CIMB ASEAN Research Institute, (2013) Lifting-the-Barriers Roundtable: Capital Markets, Network ASEAN Forum.

Shimizu, S. (2014a) *Financial Globalization and Regionalism in East Asia*, eds. Kinkyo, T., Matsubayashi, Y., and Hamori, S., Chapter "Asian Bond Markets Initiative: The way forward," (Routledge) pp. 76–97.

Shimizu, S. (2014b) ASEAN Financial and capital Markets—Policies and Prospects of Regional Integration, RIM Vol. ⅩⅣ No.54, Japan Research Institute.

Volz, U. (2013) *ASEAN Financial Integration in the Light of Recent European Experiences*, Paper prepared for a special issue of the Journal of Southeast Asian Economies, May.

Wihardja, M.M. (2013). *Financial Integration Challenges in ASEAN beyond 2015*, ERIA Discussion Paper Series, Nov.

Index

Extractive Industry Transparency
   Initiative (EITI), 175
extreme poverty, 101, 114

Factor Augmented VAR (FAVAR),
   15
FAVAR model, 16
   financial spillovers, 149, 150, 159
financial stress shock, 147, 150, 160
financialization of commodities, 32
foreign direct investment (FDI), 84

General Methods of Moments (GMM),
   86, 88, 92
genuine saving, 122
global financial crisis, 69, 78, 147
Global VAR (GVAR), 15
gold return, 32, 33, 41, 43, 55, 56
government capacity, 164, 168,
   170–172

Implementation Plan for ASEAN
   Capital Markets Integration, 190,
   191, 203
impulse response, 43, 44, 50, 63,
   71, 78
Inclusive Growth, 166, 173
inflation rate, 109, 112, 114
inflation, 91, 92
institutional quality, 170, 172
international capital flows, 60, 76, 78
international transmission of shocks,
   31, 33, 36

Kansas City Financial Stress Index
   (KCFSI), 151

large N, 128

Markov chain Monte Carlo (MCMC),
   63
Markov-switching model, 32, 37–39

Markov-switching vector
   autoregressive (MS-VAR), 61
mean group (MG), 88
MG estimators, 88, 89, 92
migration, 84
monetary policy shocks, 148, 150, 152,
   160
most countries, 60
MSIAH-VAR model, 61, 62, 67, 71,
   75, 78

national oil company, 173
natural resource fund, 166, 167
natural resource reserve, 123
non-renewable, 170

of the curse of dimensionality, 17
official development assistance (ODA),
   84
oil exporter, 122, 123, 137
oil prices, 17, 19, 21, 26
ordinary least squares (OLS), 86, 105
orthogonalized impulse response
   function (OIRF), 20
overlapping moving block bootstrap,
   153

panel data, 107, 110, 114
parts, 107
permanent income hypothesis, 170–172
PMG estimator, 88, 89, 92, 95, 97
pooled mean group (PMG), 88
poverty gap, 105, 106
poverty headcount ratio, 105–107, 114
poverty ratio, 106, 107, 112–114
price volatility, 165, 168
principal component, 37–40
procyclical, 165

Qualified ASEAN Banks, 186
quality of institutions, 122, 135
quality of investment, 122

Printed in the United States
By Bookmasters